Cover Design by Daria K. Willson
Cover Art by Armelle Dhomé.
Original water color
used by permission of the artist.

"Joie de Vivre" is a French
expression which translates
"Passion for Living"

ISBN 0-9760427-0-3

"When she greets foreign visitors at the Atlanta Airport, Mrs. Cunningham holds aloft the flags of their countries."

Joie de Vivre

A memoir of
Survival, Service, Serendipity

Rose G. Cunningham

WITH

Charles Josey

DEDICATION

This book is dedicated to the memory of

my beloved parents, Rachel and Marcel Gold,

my brother, George, my dear husband, John,

my daughters, Valerie and Marcelle, my grandchildren,

John Ryan and Ashley Anne,

and to the unborn children

who will be the future descendants

of my family.

ACKNOWLEDGEMENTS

First and foremost, my editor and friend Charles Josey for
working so hard on this book and understanding what these
pages mean to me. During the countless hours we spent together, I discovered his patience and insight on my life.

My profound gratitude to my beloved husband John, who encouraged me to write my memoirs and whose love and patience
through the years have taught me what is
important in life.

My beloved daughter Valerie for giving me so much
support and believing in me. My beloved younger daughter,
Marcelle, who also encouraged me and who kept in touch with
me despite the long distances that separate us.

Many thanks to my long time friend, Marge McDonald, for her creative ideas.

Thank you also to Stephen Stoffle and Anita Ransom
who helped me with my computer skills.

A big "Thank you," Muchas gracias," and "Merci beaucoup" to
Caroline Guest, Anna May Hirsch, Stephen Edwards and Johana Nadler
for their suggestions.

And, two wonderful ladies who came into my life,
Daria K. Willson and Carri Schwab, with their brilliant, resourceful
artistic work, and Daria's attractive cover design.

Last of all, with immense gratitude to Denese Van Dyne.

Life is real! Life is earnest!

And the grave is not its goal.

Dust thou art, to dust returnest,

Was not spoken of the soul.

Not enjoyment, and not sorrow,

Is our destined end or way;

But to act, that each tomorrow

Find us farther than today.

Let us then be up and doing,

With a heart for any fate;

Still achieving, still pursuing,

Learn to labor and to wait.

Henry Wadsworth Longfellow

A Psalm of Life

Past Present

Ashley, age 12

In 1999, I decided to take my twelve year old granddaughter, Ashley, to Port Manec'h, Brittany, France and show her the beach where I played as a twelve year old child. I wanted to find the cottage where my parents, my brother, and I spent six months.

We went to the local grocery store to ask the whereabouts of the cottage. The owner of the store looked at the picture I had brought and said, "Let me call Madame Yvette. She is 85 years old and lived here during WW II."

Madame Yvette walked slowly with her cane, but when she saw the picture she exclaimed, "This is Armelle's grandmother's house, *Ker Cri.* Soon, Armelle appeared at the store and was amazed to see her grandmother's house and dogs in my picture. Armelle Dhomé, in her early fifties, was the epitome of Parisian elegance. Her blue eyes sparkled with intelligence and her short, shiny, dark blonde hair framed a soft, beautiful face. Her grandmother, Madame Deon, was my parent's landlady who owned the cottage we rented right across the street from her house. Armelle led us to it.

After our visit to the cottage, I remembered the garden with its profusion of flowers – rhododendrons, azaleas, roses. Ashley and I took the path to the beach. Above us the sky was a stunning blue, spotted with white patches of clouds that resembled little islands. The air smelled of fish and iodine and carried a sharp coolness that awakened all my senses. Below us, the agitated Atlantic splashed fiercely onto the rocky beach.

Rose, age 12

I watched my beautiful, precocious granddaughter hurry ahead, her long chestnut hair floating in the breeze. She called back to me, "Come, show me where you used to play." "In a moment," I said, taking in her perfect oval face and big, dark brown sparkling eyes. "Some day, " she challenged me, "you must write about all this."

While Ashley ran along the narrow strip of sand that threaded down to the beach, my eyes swept across the panorama of cliffs and water at Port Manec'h, France, and a tidal wave of memories swept over me.

I was twelve again, skipping along this same path on summer camp outings and later playing there after my parents rented a nearby house. My mind flooded with fond childhood memories – as well as an event that put my entire family's existence in jeopardy.

As I joined Ashley, I tried to brush away the memory of one particular moment. On September 3, 1939, my brother George and I were at a summer camp, enjoying a picnic on this beach. Our happy meal came to an abrupt halt when news arrived that France and England had declared war on Germany, thus starting World War II. Parents were called hurriedly to come for their children, and the summer camp suddenly closed.

Sixty-two years later, in 2001, I revisited Armelle in Port Manec'h. At the exact time Armelle and I strolled that same beach, another international conflict began. In France it was afternoon; in the United States, it was the infamous morning of September 11, 2001 when four planes crashed: two into New York's famous World Trade Towers, one into the Pentagon, and another - painstakingly diverted from the U.S. Capitol - crashed in a Pennsylvania field. Once, again, the world was plagued by terror, and nothing would be quite the same anymore.

Armelle Dhomé

Air traffic was halted. For four anxious days air travel into the U.S. was forbidden.

I thought about the beach at Port Manec'h; how I was there, when twice, political and religious strife altered the course of world events and the path of my life.

Another challenge, another twist. Tragedy, sorrow, recovery and, eventually, renewal. I have experienced that cycle many times.

Regardless, I'm standing strong and tall, still pursuing my passion for life, my *Joie de Vivre*.

Part I

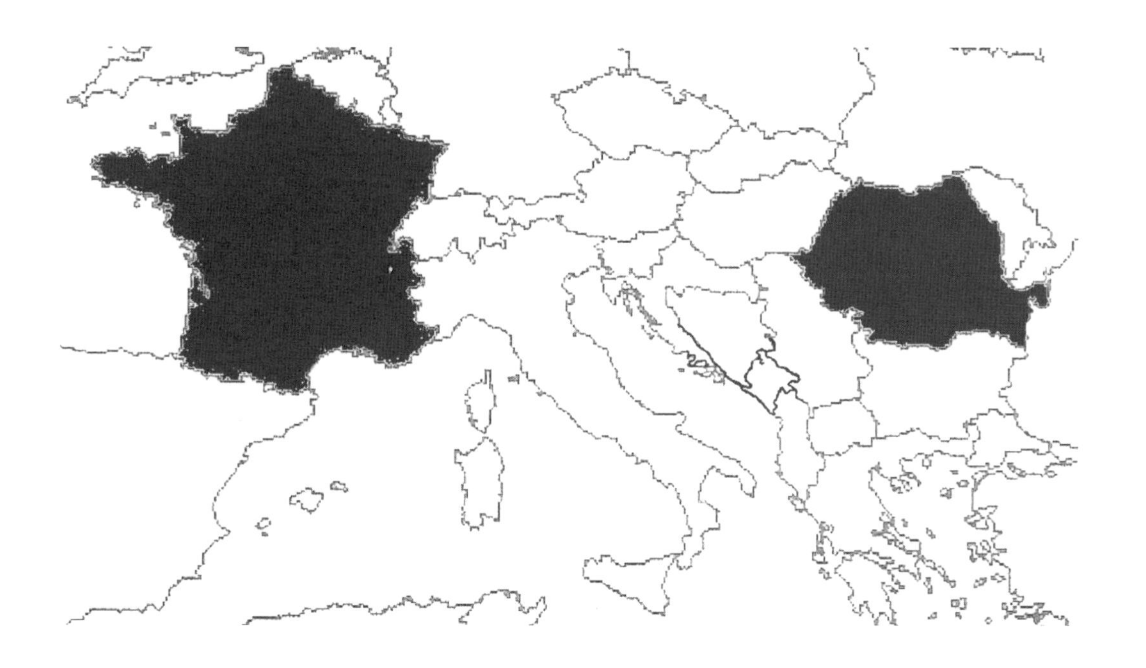

1894

That year, many events occurred that would later directly influence my life. Baron de Courbertin founded the committee to organize the modern Olympic Games, and Nicholas II, through his ineptness as a monarch, would create fertile ground for the rise of Communism, came to Russia's throne. That same year, one of the most powerful Communists of all was born: Nikita Khrushchev. The French had just lost their final opportunity to control world trade by abandoning construction of the Panama Canal amidst corruption and political upheaval that included French army Captain Alfred Dreyfus being falsely convicted of treason. It was a time when countries – especially European countries – measured their power by the number of colonies and/or protectorates they controlled and when European royalty was basking in the twilight of its glory. Prince Hohenlohe became Chancellor of Germany, while tiny Japan proved it could defeat mammoth China at Port Arthur. Scientific discovery and world-shaping inventions were happening simultaneously in separate countries. Louis Lumière and Thomas Edison independently fathered the cinema, while Yersin and Kitasato autonomously discovered the plague bacillus. The impressionist painters, such as Degas, Corbett and Caillebotte, as well as composers such as Debussy, Richard Strauss, and Sibelius were reinterpreting the world in both beautiful and horrifying works. 1894 was the year when Aldous Huxley, James Thurber, J.B. Priestley, Harold MacMillian, and my father were born.

My Parents

My passion for life was undoubtedly inherited from my father, Marcel Gold. He not only seized the smaller opportunities that came his way, he, more importantly, created major ones by employing his vision and tenacity. I believe I have done the same.

Papa, 1931

He was born March 7, 1894 in Marseilles, France, the son of a Jewish raincoat maker. That year, the bubonic plague hit Marseilles. The Black Death (as it was called) destroyed one fourth of the population of Europe, killing over ten million people between 1300 and 1899. Among those who perished in 1894 was my father's mother, Rose Gold, the lady for whom I am named. Although Papa's father survived the plague, his grief drove him to suicide, leaving little Marcel to be raised by his widowed grandmother, Sophia Apoteker.

As a young man, my father studied business at the University of Vienna. There, he became fluent in German. Over time, he mastered a total of five languages: French, German, Romanian, Spanish, and English.

Knowledge of languages opened doors for him, as it has for me. One of those doors swung wide open in 1924, when he was thirty-one. He decided to go to Romania as a trade attaché for the French Government.

By 1924, he must have amassed a certain amount of wealth; otherwise, I don't know how he could have landed a spot in the French Diplomatic Corps. Marcel Gold was certainly a brilliant man and a gifted mathematician. I remember watching him add columns of figures faster than you or I can with the aid of a calculator. My assumption is that he made a considerable amount of money in the stock market before leaving France. I do know that during his years in Romania his knowledge of the market led him to be heavily involved in it, resulting in some sound investments.

In Romania, he met Rachel Luci Rohrlich, a beautiful girl ten years his junior. A mutual acquaintance introduced them at an intermission during a performance of the Sigmund Romberg operetta *The Student Prince*. An introduction was the only way to properly meet someone in those days. It was

Mama, 1935

unthinkable for a gentleman to approach a lady he did not know and initiate conversation.

Luci Rohrlich fell hard for the handsome Frenchman and he for the elegant Romanian lady. With her father's permission, the two wed in 1924. While my father continued his work in the French Diplomatic Corps, the couple began a family. My brother George (nicknamed Gica) must have been conceived on their wedding night because he was born nine months later, on February 17th, 1925. I came into the world almost two years later, December 12th, 1927 at 5:30 p.m.

My birth certificate, which was recorded in French at the French Consulate in Bucharest, states that I was born at my parents' home, *Romulus*. The listed witnesses were my grandmother, Rebecca Rohrlich, who was then 50 years old, and my great-grandmother Sophia Apoteker, who was 70.

Another entry on the birth certificate brings up a question I cannot answer. Exactly what was my mother's name? Earlier I wrote that it was Rachel Luci, but that may or may not have been correct. My birth certificate lists her simply as Luci Gold, while her passport declares her as *Rachel Gold*. Her family and my father called her Luta, which is a diminutive of Lucia. Yet Lucia isn't a Romanian name; Luta, on the other hand, is. Was Rachel Luci her name or Luci Rachel, or was her name changed to facilitate getting a visa during the chaotic years when my family was fleeing one form of political tyranny after another? I once asked her for clarification, and she simply said, "My name is Rachel."

1927

That year, Janis Cakste, the first president of Latvia, died, as well as Ferdinand I, King of Romania. Romania crowned Ferdinand's five-year-old grandson Michael. That same year, The Iron Guard Fascists were organized in Romania, and the World War I Armistice finally became official. In Germany, Inter-Allied military control ended and the country's economic system collapsed. Trotsky was expelled from the rapidly growing Communist party, while socialists rioted in Vienna, following the acquittal of Nazis for political murder. In the United States, Henry Ford rolled his 15 millionth Model T off his assembly line. Movies became "talkies." Mickey Mouse made his debut, the Academy Awards were born, Charlie Chaplin divorced his first wife, and the stock market climbed toward giddy heights. Charles Lindbergh flew non-stop from New York to Paris in 33.5 hours, Atlanta's Bobby Jones won the U.S. Golf Association Amateur championship, Norway's Sonja Henie turned ice-skating into an international passion, and Olympic great Johnny Weissmuller swam 100 yards in 51 seconds. I.P. Pavlov published his findings on conditioned reflexes, and I was welcomed into the world by an adoring family.

Childhood in Romania

My mother was a beautiful woman, the quintessence of elegance, a lady who wore splendid hats and dresses. She had attended college and studied pharmacy in Bucharest. However, in those days, ladies did not apply their education outside the home; what she did was entertain for my father.

Then, as now, the percentage of a diplomat's achievements that took place at social functions often exceeded those that were occurring in conference rooms and offices. Many parties were held at our house, and I remember my brother Gica and myself sneaking away from our nanny to peek over the stair rail at the guests. They were always dressed to perfection, as they drank their vintage champagne, ate beluga caviar, and chatted in multiple languages.

Despite this privileged life style, Mama suffered a lot as a result of my father's continual philandering. My mother certainly wasn't the only one attracted to this tall, virile man with his piercing, dark brown eyes and a profusion of wavy, brown hair. Mama used to refer to him as "mon bel homme," which is the epitome of a very handsome man. He certainly was that long after his hair turned silver.

When I became an adult, my mother told me numerous stories. For example, once when he had gone to France on business, she decided she would surprise him by joining him in Paris. She knew the hotel where he always stayed, the famous Hotel de la Paix, which is across from the Opera. The moment she stepped off the train, Mama headed there. The hotel's equally famous café had an outdoor area that could be enclosed with glass panes in winter. Spying her husband at one of the tables, she tapped on the glass, and was he surprised! Luckily for him, when she arrived, he was sitting alone. It became evident, however, that he had to hurriedly cancel his plans for the remainder of his stay in Paris.

Aside from solo business trips, Papa did travel a great deal with Mama, especially after I entered Catholic school. Prior to that, I had a nanny and a tutor, allowing our parents to travel without leaving Gica and me alone.

George was nicknamed Gica, which is a Romanian diminutive of George. When we were children, there were also summers away at camp...separate camps, of course. We only traveled with our parents in Romania. They liked having their time apart and with other adults; however, I don't recall feeling slighted and do remember that after each trip our parents returned loaded with presents for us.

Looking back, I see George as the scapegoat of the family. While I was a little spoiled brat who was treated like a princess, he was the one who was always blamed for everything. My father picked on him unmercifully and was downright cruel to him.

However, Papa was not the only one. I also was terribly mean to George when we were young and held him in contempt, which is a terrible thing to say. He was timid and somewhat of a sissy. Perhaps that's why our father did not idolize him, as he did me. The situation hurt my mother greatly, and she would admonish me – not my father – and tell me to be nice to George, adding, "After all, he's the only brother you have." Despite my mother's pleas, it would be several years before her two children became close.

Our house in Bucharest

One of my earliest memories of the two of us occurred when I was about five years old. Our house in Bucharest had a gorgeous glass door separating the living room from the dining room. One day, George and I were playing freight train with a battery-powered car that he had been given. It was large enough to seat a child. George suggested that we pretend the glass door was the border between two countries and dared me to drive through the closed door. I did, and the door was shattered. That was the first time my father ever spanked me; however, the spanking I received was nothing compared to the one George got.

Mama's discipline was largely based on threats that, if we weren't good, the Turks would come and get us. Sometimes the threat was the gypsies. The Turks had been long time enemies of the Romanians, consequently, they were not favorably depicted to Romanian children. The gypsies, however, were a more formidable threat. I had never seen a Turk, but gypsies were another matter. Their nomadic bands were native to Romania, and while considered picturesque, they were viewed as dangerous and short on scruples. Any reference to either the Turks or the gypsies gave any child reason to improve his or her behavior.

Until I turned three, we had a German nanny who taught George and me German. Papa was already fluent in German. Today, I can understand the language but not speak it. Nonetheless, I'm certain that if I spent about three months in Germany, I could quickly pick it up again. That, however, is something I have no desire to do.

As children, we also learned Romanian and French. At my father's insistence, French was the spoken language at home. That meant my mother also had to become fluent in Papa's native tongue. If she spoke Romanian at home, my father would go into a rage. German lessons stopped when Papa fired the German nanny and replaced her with a French tutor because Papa strongly suspected that the nanny was a Nazi sympathizer. I'm certain my mother was never consulted about this matter or about many others. Marcel Gold was like a general ruling over his domain.

Ice Skating

One of my happiest childhood memories that involved my father is the frequent times when he took my cousin Florie and me ice-skating. In the winter, it was a major diversion in Romania.

My least happy childhood memory of Papa was his approach to teaching me to swim. He believed the only way to learn how was to simply do it: he threw me into the water. I almost drowned. Since then, I've hated being in the water, and I especially hate having my head under water.

When I was a child, we also used to go on winter sleigh rides. There were no taxis. We rode under heavy blankets, and the snow was very deep.

Sleigh rides in Bucharest, Romania

Another vivid memory is of an earthquake that shook Bucharest about two years before we left. The quake was enough to destroy our huge tile stove. I distinctly remember the light blue tiles, specked with white dots, rising up to the ceiling.

From the time George turned eight and was sent to a Catholic school for boys, he and I saw little of each other, except on weekends. He would come home on Saturdays, then return to school late the next day. When I turned seven, my life followed a similar pattern: I was sent to school.

Papa selected for me Santa Maria, a Catholic-run boarding school considered Bucharest's finest school for girls. The dormitory and classrooms were within a park area that was surrounded by high walls. The school uniform was all black: the cape, the dress, the stockings, and the shoes. Quite a foreboding look! Three times a day we prayed on our knees, and the total experience made a deep impression on me. For several years, I truly wanted to become a nun. I was quite entranced by the Catholic pageantry and found it beautiful.

Specifically, I remember the students being taken on outings and the dormitory where we slept. The younger girls were in a large room, and my bed was next to the tented area reserved for the nun in charge of us. At night, I had a difficult time falling asleep because I became so intrigued by the nun's process of undressing for bed. She took off layer after layer after layer of clothing and would drape each garment over the rods that supported the draperies cloistering her personal area. The fact that she wore so many types and styles of garments I had never seen before fascinated me.

During the first eleven years of my life, every Sunday lunch was at the home of my mother's parents. My mother had three sisters: Frida, Aurica, and Fany, who were late marrying and lived at home with their parents.

Rose and George, 7 and 9, in Catholic school uniforms

Incidentally, my mother was not born in the house that I knew as my grandparents' home. At the time of her birth, her parents lived in Piatra Neamtz, Romania. My maternal grandfather, the great grandson of Baron Von Rohrlich, was in the lumber business and considered upper middle class. The lumber business must have been quite lucrative because he and his family became financially able to acquire the mansion that I remember as their home. It was a grand creation filled with beautiful antiques, Persian rugs, Baccarat and Lalique crystal, Sévres china, and creations from the imaginative mind of Fabergé. Everything was the very best, and I loved going there. Since my brother and I were the only grandchildren, my grandparents and aunts lavished us with attention and absolutely adored George and me. At that time, I was not aware of the atmosphere of wealth in which I grew up. Children tend to accept their initial environment as being normal.

However, the idyllic lifestyle into which I had been born began a process of deterioration - slow at first, then accelerating rapidly. Even though both sides of my family had lived for generations as Roman Catholics (celebrating Christmas, observing the Christian holidays and sending their children to Catholic schools), my father was fired from his position with the French government when it was learned that his ancestry was Jewish. That's how strong the anti-Semitic movement was throughout Europe – especially in Romania. I regret not having been reared in a Jewish household. I missed out on the tradition.

We were not a very religious family, at least in the American sense. In the United States, religion is mixed with society and a sense of community. In Romania and throughout Europe, it was very different. We would go to church, light a candle, make a prayer and leave. There was no contact with the other people who attended the same church. Incidentally, the Roman Catholic Church was not dominant in Romania. There, most of the population attended Greek Orthodox churches.

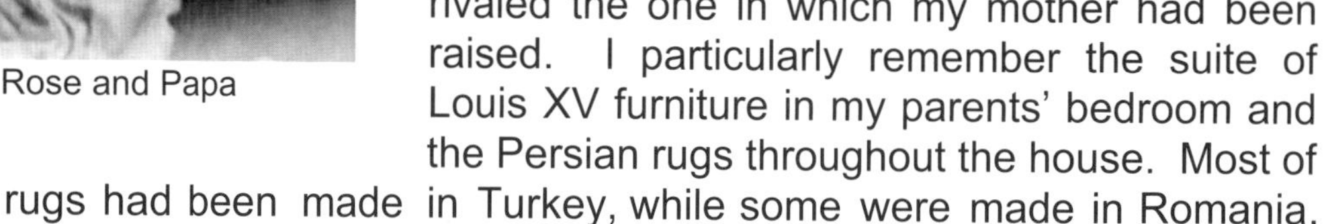

Rose and Papa

Despite being dismissed from his government position, my father decided to remain in Romania and went into banking. Simultaneously, he continued his stock investments.

Even without the diplomatic corps' social whirl, it was a good life and a privileged one. Our family had a nanny, a tutor, and a cook, as well as a gardener who tended the grounds and our vegetable garden. Our antique-filled house rivaled the one in which my mother had been raised. I particularly remember the suite of Louis XV furniture in my parents' bedroom and the Persian rugs throughout the house. Most of those rugs had been made in Turkey, while some were made in Romania, which was famous for its hand-woven rugs.

In addition to our permanent servant staff, we also had a dressmaker who came to the house to make all my clothes and some of my mother's. In those days, if you were well to do, you did not go shopping. The exception was when you traveled to various cities, such as London and Paris, where the most fashionable clothes and hats could be purchased.

When I was ten, George and I were taken out of school and taught at home by a very unattractive man with a big nose. He would come at certain hours each day, but our education was no longer structured or in any way organized. I received little or no explanation for the change, but I was full of questions. Despite (or perhaps because of) my inquisitiveness, I received no answers. George was more passive than I and didn't inquire about the changes in our lives.

It wasn't until a year later that we both knew for certain that something was going on. We knew when the men came to crate and store our furniture.

Still, my father didn't give us any details until that fateful day when we left Romania. That was when I learned why my father had been dismissed from his position with the French government. He bluntly told George and me, "We have to leave because we're Jewish. Romania will surely fall into the hands of either the Germans or the Communists. I am determined to spare all of us either fate."

That is when and how I found out. I had never heard a word about our Jewish ancestry, neither from my parents nor from my maternal grandparents. The shock, at age eleven, was enormous. And I was angry. Very angry. How could they have lied to me? I felt deceived and didn't want to be Jewish.

Having attended a Catholic school, having been taught and guided by nuns, having even wanted to become a nun – then suddenly learning that I was not who I thought I was – learning I had to leave my home and my country because of a family secret that I had never known filled me with turmoil. If things had not been moving at such a rapid pace, I'm certain it would have taken a great deal of time to get over it. In retrospect, I can understand my family's reasons for not telling us children. I do wonder, however, at what age – if any – I would have been told the truth if the political situation hadn't forced my father's hand.

Other than clothes, the only things we took with us were pictures: pictures of family, pictures of friends, and pictures of the only place I knew as home. In the blink of an eye, we lost that wonderful house. My father had sent his money to the United States, knowing it wouldn't be safe anywhere else. Having been in the diplomatic corps and banking, he had enough connections in the U.S to enable such major financial transfers. If he hadn't, I would not be alive to tell my story.

George and Mama

Later my father got word to my aunts to sell the furniture for what they could get for it and use the money for food and survival. My grandparents, being elderly and set in their ways, had refused to leave Romania. That being the case, my aunts felt they had no choice but to stay with them and see to their needs. So they stayed and sold our furnishings for the little they brought on the black market. Soon after that, my grandparents and aunts found themselves doing the same with their own magnificent possessions. Finally, they lost their lovely house to the Communists and were forced to live in a two-room apartment for the remainder of all their lives.

1939

U.S. President Roosevelt beefed up U.S. military while renouncing its Japanese trade agreement of 1911 and demanding assurances from Hitler and Mussolini that they would not attack 31 specific nations, Romania among them. While the U.S. declared itself "neutral", Germany invaded Poland while England and France declared war on Germany. The League of Nations continued to crack and crumble as Hungary and Spain pulled out, and Russia was expelled for invading Finland. Russia also had its eye on Romania. Anti-Semitism spread like a plague throughout Europe. Germany occupied Bohemia and Moravia, placed Slovakia under "protection", annexed Memel, and renounced its nonaggression pact with Poland and naval agreement with England. The British began conscription, used balloons as barriers against aircraft attacks and built radar stations to give early warning of approaching enemy planes. In the U.S., even though unions were striking and flexing their muscles, the economy was rapidly recovering, in large part due to European orders for arms and war equipment. Igor Sikorsky built the first helicopter, Paul Muller synthesized DDT, and Joliot-Curie demonstrated the possibility of splitting the atom. Pan-American Airways began regular scheduled commercial flights between the U.S. and Europe on its "Dixie Clippers", and in Atlanta, the movie *Gone with the Wind* premiered and soon swept the Academy Awards.

Leaving Romania

We made our departure in the early spring of 1939. Leaving my friends and family was quite traumatic for me. All I truly understood about our situation was that my father's word was final in this, as well as in all other matters. My mother had no more say about our leaving than George or myself. But our father was right, he knew – or at least suspected – what would happen.

In spite of the trauma of leaving the only world I had ever known, I have to admit that I was excited and initially swept up in the adventure of it all. After all, I was eleven at the time. The possible horrors of war and persecution of Jews were not real to anyone who had grown up in such a sheltered world.

We left Bucharest on the famous Orient Express. Whatever stories you might have heard about this legendary train's luxury are probably true. We boarded with our luggage, looking like a family on holiday. We had a sleeper car, but I don't think any of us got much sleep. We children were too excited over the experience of traveling on that legendary train, while the adults worried about safely reaching our destination: Paris. Both silently grieved over being separated from family, friends, and the home they had created and loved.

The train traveled from Romania, crossing Yugoslavia, and into Italy. We traveled without incident until we reached Vingtimilia, an Italian town on the border of Italy and France. Having crossed other borders without incident, we were not prepared for what happened when the French authorities came on board to check passports.

They saw that my mother's passport listed her as a native of Romania, while my father's listed him as French. These border guards said that my father, George, and I could continue to France; however, my mother could not because she was Romanian. Papa told them that she had frequently traveled to France with him and had even gone alone. Furthermore, he had a diplomatic passport. The guards did not budge. Their explanation was that "things had changed" and France might go to war. Therefore, she had to have a visa to enter France. My father's persistence got us nowhere. Finally, he was told that we would have to go to Rome to apply for the visa at the French Embassy.

Seeing that there was no other option, we collected our luggage, transferred to another train, and headed for Rome. We arrived at night, checked into a hotel, and then went to the French Embassy the next morning. Papa had no problem acquiring Mama's visa, and we caught the next train back to Vingtimilia, where we were allowed to cross the border into Modano, France and proceed to Paris.

I have particularly vivid memories of this part of the trip. Once we crossed the border, the scenery rapidly changed. The world we had left was deep in snow, but upon entering France, it was spring. The trees and flowers were beginning to blossom. lit was a glorious sight.

Something else was blossoming: a new relationship between George and me. We were no longer living separate lives and for some years to come would seldom be with other children long enough to establish friendships. Gradually we became quite close, and I am glad we did.

Throughout the trip – even the detour to Rome – we traveled first class. However, once we arrived in Paris, the luxury stopped, and my father transformed from being the big spender into the most frugal person imaginable. For example, instead of heading for his usual home away from home, Hotel de la Paix, we checked into the dingy L' Hôtel Paris-Centre, where the elevators were more often out of commission than not and opulence was in short supply. Papa did, however, take two rooms. George and I shared one, while my parents occupied the other.

Life in France

While we were in Paris, my father continued his attempts at purchasing us visas that would allow him to take us away from Europe and its troubles. He spent days going from one embassy to another, trying to purchase the precious legal documents for all of us. At that time, selling visas was a lucrative source of income for most countries. Unfortunately for my family, the United States was not one in the business of selling. Papa went to the embassies for all the South American countries but had no luck. He even tried to get us to Hong Kong, South Africa, New Zealand, or Australia. Anywhere outside of Europe became his goal and the process occupied him full time.

Sensing that it was not going to be a rapid process, he moved us from the hotel to a furnished apartment in St. Cloud, which was a great improvement in our living conditions. However, he kept assuring us that the apartment would also be temporary. Even though war had not reached France, he believed it would and was eager to move his family to a safer place.

When the summer of 1939 arrived, we still had no visas. Papa decided George and I should get out of the city and experience some of the beauty of his native country; so, he sent us both to a summer camp in Brittany's Port Manec'h, a tiny village atop rugged cliffs that overlook the ocean. It is located in the province of Finistère, which translates, *end of the earth.* Considering my recollection of how long it took to get there from Paris, I felt it was well named. When we eventually stepped off that train, I began the happiest time of my childhood. My father could not have selected a place that we could have enjoyed more.

Port Manec'h, Brittany, France, circa 1940

Unlike the camps we had attended in Romania, there were both boys and girls at this camp, about fifteen in all, ranging in age from eleven to fourteen. There were three girls or three boys per room. The house was big but certainly not what one would call a chateau. Furthermore, it was not as large as I recalled. When I saw the house again, years later, I didn't recognize it because I remembered it being much larger. As adults, we look at things with different eyes.

The tall, full bosomed lady who ran the camp was called Tante Miche. This plump, jolly woman made a great impression on me. She was motherly, sweet, and very concerned about our welfare. The staff consisted of Tante Miche, her sister (who was joint owner of the house), a cook, and a cleaning woman.

Until that fall, there were no major events affecting my daily life at camp. Our life was not structured. The days were filled with walks in the countryside, painting parties, games with my new friends, hide-and-seek in the house's large garden, which was my favorite past-time, and basking in the care that Tante Miche lavished on us youngsters. There were numerous day trips to nearby sites, trips Tante Miche considered educational, as well as entertaining. She was correct on both accounts. I clearly remember our visits to the beach, as well as to a nearby farm where we saw butter and cider made. Brittany's cider is unlike any other in the world. To this day, I still love its taste.

The people of Brittany were also uniquely individual. The elderly spoke their own language – Breton, not French as Tante Miche did – and did not consider themselves part of France.

Brittany, it seems, can be hot, cool, humid and dry at the same time. But, unlike Paris, the region does not get bitterly cold in winter. The third of September, 1939, was one of those balmy days of kaleidoscope weather. We children, were on the beach having a picnic when chilling news arrived - France was now at war with Germany.

Tante Miche herded us back up the path to the camp and began calling all the parents to come fetch their children. Our summer of bliss had ended. George and I were the last to leave because Papa had told Tante Miche that, at the end of camp, he and Mama planned to come to Brittany for a vacation. And - they did come, more in search of safety than anything else.

My parents rented a small cottage with a view of the ocean. Unlike most of the houses in the area, which were low and whitewashed with thatched roofs, our small cottage had two stories. It also had a lovely rose garden that my mother especially enjoyed. A steep, winding path led to that small beach where the sound of the surf was like the beat of nature's heart. The pungent smell of the sea became entrenched in my memory.

It was just the four of us there, no servants, just us. My mother had to learn to cook, and we had fresh fish every day. The fishermen traveled door to door so that the housewives could make a selection from their daily catch. I never ate so much fresh tuna in my whole life. What we couldn't eat on the day of purchase had to be salted or smoked for preservation because there was no electricity in Port Manec'h, consequently no refrigerators.

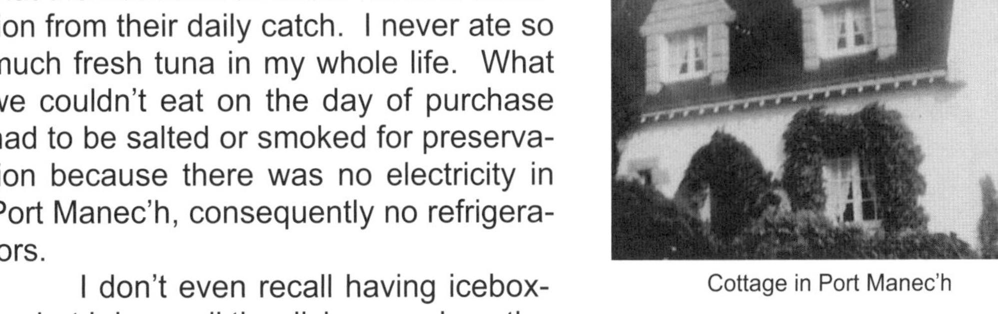
Cottage in Port Manec'h

I don't even recall having iceboxes, but I do recall the dishes, such as the region's specialty, savory crepes called *gallettes.* These delicious buckwheat pancakes were filled with eggs, ham, cheese, smoked tuna, or salmon, and were usually washed down with home-brewed cider. The other local beverage was Brittany's popular Muscadet wine. You found it on every home's table and in every local café. I also soon learned to appreciate the Breton cakes, which were made from brioche dough. They were usually served warm, smelled divine, and tasted heavenly.

Even with the war drawing closer and closer to French soil, my life was filled with a brief span of joy. My father bought secondhand bicycles for George and me. While riding my bicycle on the uneven roads, I discovered a succession of striking landscapes where the cliffs and rocks were worn into strange shapes by the persistent waves and by creeks on their way to join them.

Every day George and I peddled to the bakery in Pont-Aven, the next town, to buy fresh bread because Port Manec'h had no bakery. Even as youngsters, it was impossible for us to ignore the beauty of the area. We may not have seen it as Paul Gauguin did when he came there to paint, but it was still our Eden. On our first trip to the bakery, the warm, aromatic bread smelled so good, George and I polished off the entire loaf before we got back to the cottage. From then on, we were given enough money to buy an extra loaf as our special treat on the return trip.

In our travels, George and I were a bit bewildered to discover that some of the older neighbors spoke Breton, a Celtic language similar to Welsh and Cornish, which was totally foreign to us. The local priest, a tall and slender man with infinitely warm eyes and breath that always smelled of garlic, explained to us the reason for this strange spoken language.

He often visited our cottage and took great pleasure in adding to George's and my knowledge of local history. In his deep, melodious voice, he explained to us that in the first centuries A.D., the Bretons spoke a form of Gallic that they brought from the British Isles. So, the area's language began as a form of Gallic that, over time, changed, as all languages do. Several centuries after the Bretons' arrival, Bretagne or Brittany (known as Armorica to the Romans) became part of the Roman Empire. Combined, these situations impeded the development of the French language in Brittany, and many of the elderly stubbornly held onto what they regarded as their native tongue.

Adding to this was the fact that Bretons are fierce individualists who dislike the Parisians, considering them arrogant, rude, and untrustworthy. It's an opinion shared by many Americans today. My family presented total confusion for these people. It was true that we arrived from Paris, but we were not Parisians – not even French.

My father, being from Marseilles, spoke with that city's singsong accent, and my mother had a soft Romanian accent that could melt an iceberg. We children spoke with our own accent, which was a fusion of our parents' accents and the influence of Parisian schools. In short order, the locals shrugged the entire matter of accents off and welcomed us into their community. Of them all, our landlady, Madame Deon, was the kindest person in town.

Later, I learned that this dear lady, who lived across from the cottage she rented to us, was Charles De Gaulle's first cousin. And, many years later, I discovered that her descendants had inherited her kindness and hospitable nature.

I recall the cottage we rented as being a wonderful place because it was where I spent nearly all day in the company of my parents and brother. I learned so much about Brittany. We went to the farms so that we children could learn how cheese was made and crops were harvested.

My father even bought me a pair of clogs, the wooden shoes that were typically worn in the region. While I considered them a novelty, a special treat, it was likely that I wore them because of a shortage of leather shoes, due to rationing. There was a bonding among us that I hadn't experienced before and still cherish. In spite of my happy memories of life at the cottage, I also remember the daily routine of catching a mouse in our traps. It was always the highlight of our day in a country at war.

Next door to us was a family with two small children with whom George and I played. As a family, we attended the local church services, weddings, and festivities. When Christmas came, we celebrated it, as well. But, the Christmas of 1939 would be the only one we enjoyed there. Here we were, a family that had thought of itself as Christian for generations, but we had a Jewish ancestry that could lead to our deaths.

1940

While Americans sang "It's A Big, Wide Wonderful World", and marveled at the first stereophonic sound movie (Disney's *Fantasia*), Germany invaded Norway, Denmark, Holland, Belgium, and Luxembourg, and Italy declared war on France and Britain. Germany marched thousands of Jews to concentration camps and gas chambers, intensified U-boat warfare, began all-night raids on London, and bombed Manchester. The Eighth Army under Wavell opened offensive in North Africa. The Germans invaded Paris, June 14th, and Churchill offered France union with Britain, but the new head of the French government, Maréchal Pétain, signed an armistice with Germany. Trotsky was assassinated in Mexico on orders from Stalin; Howard Florey developed penicillin as a practical antibiotic; Ernest Hemingway published *For Whom the Bell Tolls*; Thomas Wolfe's *You Can't Go Home Again* was published posthumously; the cream of European composers fled to the U.S.; Matisse painted "The Romanian Blouse"; the prehistoric wall paintings in France's Lascaux caves were discovered; and the first electron microscope was demonstrated.

Flight From Paris

After six months in Brittany, we returned to Paris in February of 1940, and rented another furnished apartment. War was in progress, and there were constant reminders. At the public school that George and I attended, there were daily drills with gas masks. The French were afraid that the Germans were going to bomb with gas; however, the Germans restricted their use for the concentration camps. Still, who could predict where a nation that dealt in genocide and oppression drew the line? Another constant reminder - big posters and banners throughout the streets - claimed that France would overcome because of the existence of the Maginot Line. It was considered impenetrable.

That optimism, however, proved to be a joke. When the Nazis were ready to claim France as theirs, they simply went around the Maginot Line and entered France through Belgium. This fortified line of defense along the eastern border of France and Germany consisted of above-ground forts, pillboxes, and barbed-wire entanglements, as well as below-ground bunkers that contained every necessity from hospitals to living quarters.

In stark contrast to our half a year in Brittany, fear became a routine part of our life in Paris. I remember the bombing raids starting. When the sirens sounded, we would flee to somewhere considered safe. A subway station was not far from our apartment. That was where we usually went.

June 13, 1940, was the day before the Germans invaded Paris. It was cloudy, gray and raining... as if Paris was crying. We, along with thousands of others, were at the railway station, trying to board trains that might take us to a safer place. It was terrifying. It was pandemonium. People were running and pushing. I was afraid I would be trampled.

My father's goal was to get us onto a train headed south for Bordeaux. That wasn't easy. Thousands abandoned hope of getting on board and fled the city on bicycles. Somehow Papa managed to get us on the train. This trip, however, was a far cry from our journey on the Orient Express. People were packed in the train cars. The lucky ones got a seat - the rest stood. Once on the train, people were tense and seldom spoke. You could smell fear in the air.

When we reached Bordeaux, everyone had to leave the train, due to the heavy bombardment. Papa had the presence of mind to tell Mama, George and me to take our suitcases with us. We had not packed much. Our bags were reasonably light. Everyone hurried down some stairs that were pointed out to us by an official. The steps led to the metro tunnels. There we stayed, while bombs rained down from above. We were sure that this was it, the end for us. Bombs fell. Roofs collapsed. There was total chaos. But the tunnel roof held.

We thought the Germans were dropping the bombs, but that wasn't the case. It was the British. They were trying to destroy the tracks and hold back the Germans from sweeping through France.

During the raid, I remember one man lit a cigarette. When he did, another snatched it away from him and stomped out the ash. He accused the man of being a Nazi informer who was trying to signal the Germans with the smell from the cigarette, letting them know where we were. A big fight broke out. Hysteria reigned.

I doubt that a single cigarette could be detected over the smell of the station burning above us. Mama's face was ashen with fear. Papa clenched and unclenched his hands until they were blood red. George and I trembled in silence. Youth's feeling of immortality was gone for George and me, and we were all certain that this was the end, that our lives were over. The horror was all consuming. It remains as vivid in my mind as if I were in that metro tunnel yesterday.

For several hours, we huddled in that underground passageway, surrounded by the wounded and the dead. It was dark outside before anyone ventured out of the bomb shelter. Along with others, we began to walk away from the rubble of the city and into the countryside. The bags we originally thought were so light became heavier and heavier. We children were pleading to stop and rest, but our father insisted that the four of us push on until we found a farmhouse.

Eventually, we did spot one and headed toward it. Papa knocked on the door and explained our plight to the farmer. He also told him that we had money and would gladly pay for a place to hide and sleep. That night, we made our beds on the hay that was stored in the farmer's barn.

He and his family were very kind and moved the four of us into a room in the back of their house. There we stayed for what was probably no more than a week; however, it seemed a long, long time. Each day, my father would walk to the nearest village, Créon, to gather information. How close were the Germans? What was the safest route to the coast? Was there a train or bus we could take? Would we have to walk?

The day Papa returned with the news that he had spotted a German soldier in the town, he told Mama, "They are here. We have to leave." In preparation for the next leg of our journey, my mother cut my hair and dressed me like a boy. And that same night, the farmer told us that if we stayed, his family would be in serious trouble for hiding Jews. Since we were placing his family in danger, too, we would have to leave.

The farmer did, however, help us. He found us a broken down car and a tank of gas, then he saw us on our way. My father was a terrible driver, having always had a chauffeur to take us where we needed to go. Even so, his erratic driving and the wreck of a car got us as far as the outskirts of Marseilles.

That was the last car Papa ever owned and the last he ever drove. From the point where we abandoned the car, we walked into the city. All of us felt much safer in Marseilles because it was a demarcation zone. While we had no way of knowing at the time, it would be another year before the Germans ignored the zoning. Immediately following the Japanese attack on Pearl Harbor, December 7, 1941, the United States entered the war and the Germans invaded the rest of France.

When we arrived in Marseilles, we found France's second oldest city swarming with Jews, all trying to find a means of escape from France. Some took off on foot, climbing the Pyréneés Mountains in their attempt to reach Spain. Some managed to get passage on ships leaving the port. Others, including the four of us, waited and hoped for a means to escape.

Marseilles Park
Jewish families would arrange to reunite at this location, and meet to exchange information.

My father, having grown up in Marseilles, had contacts there, and he wasted no time in making the most of his connections. One of his contacts was an organization that was attempting to relocate Jews. Through them, he found us an apartment. At that point, anything with a roof looked good. This apartment was a one-room affair in the attic of a house on Rue Adolf Thiers.

As a child, I failed to appreciate the dingy attic apartment or the centuries of history surrounding us. Since the city's founding in the Sixth Century BC by Greek sailors from Phoenicia, this port had been the rival of Carthage and became the protector of Rome. To me, it was simply the port city that might provide our escape from Europe. We were banking on the fact that, for twenty-six centuries, Marseilles had been open to the entire world. Escaping via its port was our only chance of getting out of harm's way.

A stray cat that was as hungry as we were took up with George and me. For us, the creature was a great diversion. My father was not as enchanted with it as we were: "Here we are hungry, and you give our food to a damn cat."

Our other diversion was playing on the roofs of the buildings in our neighborhood. The houses were connected. You could easily move from roof to roof. There we met other children. It was very dangerous play, but it was what children there were allowed to do.

Rose's Cat; Rooftops behind

George was involved in something else dangerous, and I'm not quite certain why my parents allowed him to do it. He distributed the French Underground newspaper. If he had been caught, I imagine the consequences would have been severe for him, as well as the rest of the family.

Journal clandestin français reproduit par le Service des Publications de la France Combattante

"FRANCE D'ABORD!"

N° 20 - 15 MARS 1943 -

Ne partez pas vers l'Allemagne
Pour que la France meure !

Rejoignez le combat des
Partisans de Savoie,
Pour que vive la France !

"France d'Abord" est l'organe d'information, de liaison et de combat des détachements de Francs-Tireurs et Partisans qui forment, sur le sol de la Patrie l'avant-garde armée de la France Combattante.

VIVE LES VOLONTAIRES DE LA LIBERATION

La "Kollaboration" est à son comble ! Tous les Français valides sont requis afin de travailler ou se faire tuer pour que l'Allemagne hitlérienne, saignée à l'Est, puisse encore tenter de conserver ses conquêtes au nombre desquelles figure une France condamnée à sombrer dans l'esclavage !

Et sentant venir l'heure du règlement de comptes, la monstrueuse bande des Boches-Pétain, des escarpes lavaliennes, ne pense plus qu'à gagner du temps avec le sang français et à abriter sa lâcheté derrière une milice de guerre civile recrutée dans les égoûts de la trahison. Aspects de crise, mais symptômes de la décomposition mortelle des forces de l'ennemi.

C'est l'heure pour la France blessée de se lever rugissante pour frapper d'un même bras terrible !

Et la voici qui se dresse ! Les francs-tireurs dans leurs combats longtemps méconnus ont montré le meilleur des exemples. Maintenant, voici que, reprenant l'uniforme de soldat refusant la honte de repartir chez l'ennemi pour prolonger la guerre, d'autres patriotes ont répondu à l'appel aux armes en gagnant les montagnes de Savoie.

S'emparent d'un fort ici, ailleurs, se retranchant, ils ont commencé une autre forme de la guerre de libération ! Groupés en cohorte de fer, retenant des troupes ennemies, galvanisant les Français qui attendaient encore qu'on agisse pour eux :

SALUT AUX HEROS DE NOTRE SAVOIE !

Quoi que fassent entre eux les bandits de Hitler, Mussolini, Laval, les Volontaires de Savoie ont, avec les F.T.P., donné l'élan irréductible à la formation sur le sol national de la nouvelle armée française de la libération.

Mais, il faut agir, agir pour que partout surgissent les hommes en armes et le combat audacieux. Il faut combiner l'action des volontaires en formations compactes de partisans dans toutes les régions où le terrain le permet, avec l'action de harcèlement des groupes de Francs-Tireurs dissimulés, partout, à la ville comme à la campagne, de Marseille au Marais Poitevin, des Corons du Nord aux pinèdes des Landes, aux Pyrénées.

SUITE AU VERSO .....

COMMUNIQUE N° 24 DES F.T.P.F.

Pour les informations reçues entre le 1er et le 15 Mars 1943, nous relevons particulièrement les actions ci-après: Les groupes de combat appartenant aux détachements mobiles du bataillon des Alliés, en l'honneur du 25è Anniversaire de l'Armée Rouge, ont organisé une action importante qui a donné les résultats suivants :

Des déraillements importants ont eu lieu à : BEARD (ligne de Nevers à Chagny), un train de permissionnaires allemands, 52 morts, 100 blessés, voie obstruée pendant 36 heures. A SUILLY (Nièvre), train de marchandises, plusieurs wagons et 1 loco détruits. A URZY (ligne Nevers-Clamecy, qui dessert aciéries et usines chimiques), 1 loco et 15 wagons de matériel détruits.

A BRIARE (ligne Nevers-Paris), 8 wagons de matériel, une loco détruits, arrêt du trafic 48 heures. A MOULIN S/YERRE, (ligne Bourges-Sancoins), 1 train, 22 wagons vides et 1 loco détruits, voie obstruée 30 heures. A DOUZY (ligne Cosne-Clamecy), un train de matériel allemand, dégâts très importants. Trois de ces opérations ont eu lieu sur des voies surveillées par des requis civils et des garde-voies.

Les grues des dépôts de Bourges et Vierzon avaient été sabotées - deux déraillements prévus ont échoué. Le 14 une loco saute sur la plaque tournante du dépôt de BOURGES, 7 locos ne peuvent sortir pendant 20 heures.

Le 5 Mars, à SAINT CYR (Loiret), déraillement d'un train de matériel allemand partant en Russie, 2 locomotives et 20 wagons détruits dont plusieurs chargés d'explosifs et d'essence. Des câbles électriques abattus ont provoqué un incendie consumant tout le chargement - Arrêt du trafic sur 2 voies pendant 6 jours - A LA CHAPELLE SAINT-MESMIN, un train de matériel a déraillé fin Février - dégâts importants, 1 loco détruite. A FRANCOEUIL (I-&-L), 3 cuves de 150 hectolitres d'alcool chacune ont été vidangées.

VOIR SUITE AU VERSO .....

APRES UNE ACTION...

Un F.T.P. blessé, pourchassé, frappe à une porte.... Un juge l'accueille, le soigne. Merci ! Cette union du Franc-Tireur et du Juge Français, c'est la France qui retrouve son glaive pour chasser l'ennemi et punir les traîtres!

VIVE L'UNION DE GAULLE-GIRAUD !

VIVE L'UNION DE TOUS LES FRANCAIS, CONTRE LES BOCHES ET LES TRAITRES.

11

When the summer of 1941 arrived, Papa found a summer camp that was still in operation in Gap, which is in the French Alps; so, George and I were sent there. Our father knew that, in the country, we would have more and better food than he and Mama were able to find in the city, and he wanted us in a safer place. No one knew how long it might be before the Nazis ignored Marseilles' demarcation zone status and stormed the city.

Summer Camp, Gap, France

This camp was at a chateau situated on an expanded farm in the French Alps, near Gap. The lady in charge set about in earnest to put some meat on my bones. I was extremely undernourished because there was never enough food for us to eat in Marseilles. Food in all the cities was rationed. For example, we were allowed one egg per person *per month!* The little meat we received was horsemeat, and its scarcity made it a delicacy. There was no butter available, only margarine. I hated the taste of that greasy stuff, and to this day, I refuse to eat margarine. The milk we could get in the city was equally unappealing. But, at summer camp, food was plentiful because it was grown right there.

On the day we packed to return to Marseilles, the dear lady who ran the camp, Madame Louise, said she had a present for me: a dozen eggs. We all knew that the police were searching the trains for food being smuggled into the city. Their goal was to keep it from being sold on the black market. Of course, food did make its way via the black market, and I know that my mother bought what she could get.

She bought it with 1902 gold Napoleons, which were valued in 1902 at twenty francs, a considerable sum of money at that time, especially since the coins were gold. During any war, paper money is worth little or nothing, but gold holds its value. With her collection of gold coins, each worth as much as a peasant might earn in a year, Mama bought us as much as she could.

Rose wearing her Mother's Gold coin.

Ultimately, only four of her coins were not traded for food. Today, my daughters and my granddaughter each have one of them. The fourth is in a gold pendant, which I wear every day to remind me of Mama. She is with me.

Inspectors or no inspectors, portly Madame Louise, who was blessed with a sunny disposition and a determined nature, had an idea she was certain would work, an idea that could sneak my entire dozen eggs past the watchful eyes of the inspectors. She took the socks I had packed and unrolled them. In each, she placed an egg and rolled the single sock to look as if it were a pair. In that way, all twelve eggs were packed in my little suitcase.

Sure enough, the French police came on board to inspect all packages and luggage. When I was ordered to open my suitcase, my heart was beating so hard, I'm sure they could hear it. The inspector looked at the rows of socks and said, "For one little girl, you certainly have a lot of socks," and closed the suitcase.

He may well have known what I was doing and just let me get away with it. At any rate, all twelve eggs arrived in Marseilles, fresh and unbroken. My mother took them out, one by one, and put them in a plate on the table. Then we all danced around the table. Having a dozen eggs was reason to celebrate.

By that time, my parents had acquired a tiny short wave radio, although owning one to listen to the news from BBC in London was strictly forbidden. When my father needed to check the news, George would scout the street below for police. This is how we learned of the attack on Pearl Harbor on December 7, 1941, which was my mother's birthday.

1942

"The Voice of America" begins broadcasting and fills the minds and ears of the world with the news that: the Allied forces describe themselves as the "United Nations", the first American troops arrive in Europe, and the Battle of Midway rages. Despite excellent news broadcasting (and propaganda), the Voice has no means on reporting on some stories, such as the July 9th disappearance of the Frank family into an attic over an Amsterdam office; or the coded message Enrico Fermi sends to Franklin Delano Roosevelt when he initiates the first self-sustaining nuclear chain reaction for the Manhattan Project. Within two weeks of each other, Anne Frank goes into hiding, the French Vichy government rounds up tens of thousands of Jews for imprisonment in the Velodrome, and the "cleansing" of the Warsaw ghetto begins. America is lulled into a sense of security and the dream of a "White Christmas" by the smooth, soothing voice of Bing Crosby. Walt Disney releases *Bambi*- a story that speaks on the themes of unjust death, plucky perseverance, and friendship across species. Bergman, Bogey, and little Rose Gold are (either physically or fictitiously) in *Casablanca.*

En Route to Cuba

In March of 1942, on a cold damp day, my father came running up the stairs to our tiny apartment. He was out of breath and elated as he shouted, "I've got it! I've got it!"

He had, at last been able to purchase visas from the Cuban Consulate in Marseilles, as well as a ship passage to Cuba. For this, he had had to pay over a thousand dollars per person. That sum might not sound like a great deal today; however, at that time, a thousand dollars could buy you a house in the States – not a mansion, but it was a reasonable sum to pay for, say, a nice three bedroom bungalow.

Additionally, I am told that a cash deposit had to be made by each refugee family. The money was placed in a Havana bank as a "guarantee" that the family would not become a burden on the Cuban government. I assume Papa had to pay the fee; however, I have no knowledge of any such deposit ever being returned to him.

Despite the Cuban government's greed and corruption, the money Papa paid out was well spent. It bought us passage to sail with hundreds of other Jewish refugees to Cuba, via Casablanca. We sailed on the *Alhambra*, a Spanish freighter. It was to be the *Alhambra's* last trip from Marseilles to Casablanca to take Jews across the dangerous Straits of Gibraltar to their first stop on the way to freedom.

Our next ship, the *Santa Maria*, was also making her final voyage for the purpose of transporting Jews to Cuba. I don't like thinking about what our fate would have been if we had not been able to escape France. The infamous Vichy French Government sent the more than eighty thousand French Jews we left behind to concentration camps and ultimately to their deaths.

It was raining on the 8th of March when we boarded with our belongings, which were by then, very few. The men and women were separated and assigned bunks. George went with our father, while I went with our mother. Any sense of relief we felt over leaving France was short. To leave the Mediterranean, we had to sail through the Straits of Gibraltar to reach our initial destination, Casablanca.

This was a dangerous trip because the Germans had mined the narrow passage between Europe and Africa. Any ship passing through it took serious chances. In case we hit a mine, all passengers had to remain on deck, wearing life preservers. We were fortunate that cold night; our captain managed to steer us a safe course.

The next morning, when we arrived in Casablanca, the warm climate was a wonderful relief from the freezing February night we had spent on deck. As soon as the ship docked, we came down the gangplank and were taken to a building that was much like a dormitory. My father had paid extra for this special treatment. There, we ordered a meal. For each of us, it was a twelve-egg omelet – yes, a dozen eggs for each of us – followed by fresh fruits, the likes of which we had not experienced for a very long time.

Casablanca, which literally means *white house*, more than lived up to its name. Whitewashed houses filled your view in any direction. To my young mind, Casablanca was like heaven, a beautiful place with Arabs in their exotic fezzes and caftans, moving about the colorful city. Many of the peddlers carried baskets of fragrant tropical fruits. There, you would never have thought that a war was raging.

A week after our arrival in Casablanca, we boarded the Santa Maria, the Portuguese freighter that would take us to Cuba. Like the Alhambra, our previous ship, there was no hint of luxury. The men and women were restricted to separate sleeping quarters for the duration of the six-week trip; however, they were not restricted to separate areas of the ship during the day.

The winter seas were rough, and there was much seasickness. I was sick in an additional way. I had contracted a lung infection that was the early stages of tuberculosis and had to have constant care. Therefore, I spent most of my time in the infirmary, with my mother by my side. This, in a strange way, was an advantage for me because I received better food than what was served to the other passengers. Furthermore, it was neater and cleaner in the infirmary than it was below with all the other people. My parents spent as much time with me as they were allowed; however, George was not permitted to enter the infirmary.

Our first port of call was Kingston, Jamaica. When we docked, we were all taken off the ship because the Jamaican authorities believed that the passengers were hoarding gold and jewelry. Apparently, they had every intention of confiscating the valuables before the Cuban authorities had a chance to do the same. They knew that the Jews on that ship were very rich – or had been before the war. My parents, however, were down to the few gold coins Mama had left. Somehow, she managed to keep them hidden from the inspectors. The remainder of Papa's money was still secure in American banks.

While this search was in progress, I was taken to the hospital in Jamaica but was returned to the ship before it sailed. As sick as I was, I clearly recall the harbor, which was walled in by incredibly high mountains. And, I remember the smell of the tropical flowers that bloomed in profusion there, as well as the black vendors who roamed the docks, selling hats, trinkets, flowers, and fruit. The vendors chattered away in English, a language that was then as foreign to me as if they had been speaking in their native African tongues. Although, we were only 90 miles from Cuba, I felt as if I were no closer to our destination than I was in Morocco.

Our next stop was Vera Cruz, Mexico, which shared the smells and flavor of Jamaica, as well as its heat and humidity. There, as soon as I was moved to the hospital, my mother sent a telegram to King Carol II of Romania. He and his mistress Madame Lupesco were in exile in Mexico and had set up residence there, following King Carol's stormy ten-year reign. His son, Michael, had been restored to the throne but was nothing more than a figurehead for The Fascists. The telegram Mama sent explained our situation, including my illness, and asked if there was anything he could do that would enable us to stay in Mexico, rather than go on to Cuba. Unfortunately, we never heard from him; so, we had no choice except to sail on to Havana.

On our arrival in Havana's harbor, the site of the infamous bombing of the U.S.S. Maine, all five hundred of us passengers on board the converted freighter gathered on the deck, anxious to catch a glimpse of what we anticipated being our new home. But, some would see no more than the entrance to Havana's harbor and the Morro Castle lighthouse rising above the rocky cliffs because the ship was not allowed to dock.

The police sailed out and came on board to announce that the law had changed. They said the visas everyone had paid dearly to get were no longer valid. We had to pay more. As I recall, the additional amount was the equivalent of about five hundred dollars per person. My father wired the United States for the money - he had no choice. It took six months for it to arrive. During that time we were taken ashore in tenders and placed in a camp with other refugees whom the authorities believed could raise enough funds to pay the new extortion fee.

But not everyone had the resources to lay hands on more money. The people with no prospects of payment were kept on the freighter, which was about to return to Europe. Even though a number of them were old and feeble, some decided to jump ship and try swimming ashore rather than return to perish in concentration camps. Their efforts were in vain, All of the refugees who jumped ship drowned in the harbor. The chaos, the hysteria, I will never forget.

Tiscornia

For six months, we remained in a camp called Tiscornia. The place was nice, more like a summer camp than anything. We lived in dormitory style, the men on one side, the women on the other. It was the only way they could accommodate the number of people stranded there. After spending more time in the hospital, I was taken to the camp.

When I arrived, I discovered that the inhabitants of the camp included people other than those from our ship. There were also French Jews there who had sailed on ships that left much earlier than the Santa Maria, as well as ships that had sailed from Belgium and Holland and other European countries.

At the camp, these refugees had organized a children's school, which I attended when I was able. The refugees who taught us were not ordinary in any sense. They were people who had made something of their lives while in Europe and greatly valued education. All the classes they taught were conducted in French. In addition to arithmetic and the other basic courses offered to us, I distinctly remember one of the teachers who was an authority on Greek mythology. He made his classes the most memorable, and I loved the stories he told us and had us read. There was also a fantastic library that had been created by the refugees donating or lending the books they had brought with them.

The School children of Tiscornia

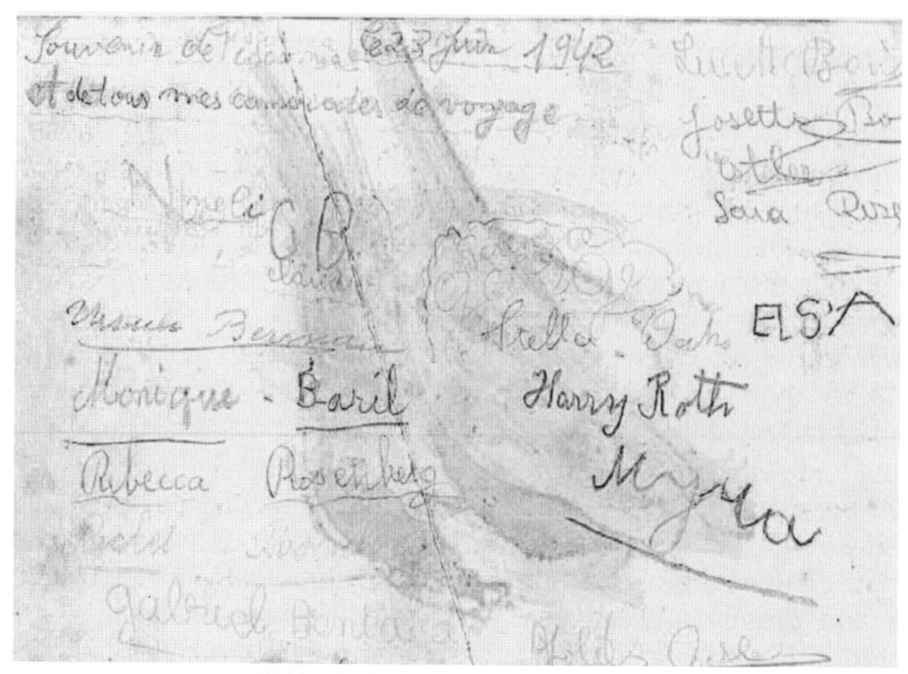

Chidren's signatures on back of photo

Looking back and realizing how few belongings any of us managed to take along, those books had to have been greatly treasured by their owners to be included in the scarce possessions they chose to bring. To share them with others was a most generous act. All the classics were included in this library, and I read and read and read the works of Tolstoy, Dickens, Shakespeare, Victor Hugo, and the best from every country. Alexander Dumas' *The Count of Monte Cristo* was my favorite. Through my reading, I received a thorough grounding in the classics, the likes of which few twelve-year-old children received then – much less now.

Bit by bit, my health improved. The collective treatments of the doctors among the refugees and the Cuban doctors, along with my personal fortitude, managed to defeat the beginnings of tuberculosis that had been plaguing me. I overheard one of the doctors say that I couldn't possibly live past age fifty. I have most certainly proven him wrong. However, for a very long time after the infection was under control and eventually cured, I remained a very skinny child.

Outside of classes and contact with my family, there was limited socializing during our half-year stay at Tiscornia. Suspicion is something you acquire when you live on the run, and it had tainted all our lives. We learned to live alone while being in a crowd. That was the safest approach to life after we left Paris for the final time. While we did make some friends after leaving France, relationships were always guarded and cautious.

I distinctly remember the garden that was adjacent to the camp, actually a rose farm that supplied the city of Havana. While the garden was strictly off limits to the refugees, I, like my father, was inquisitive and believed – and still believe – that rules are made to be broken. So, on the sly, I visited the garden two or three times a week. I always went alone, never feeling the need to do things in a group.

In truth, the other children and I didn't get along very well. I felt different. Part of the difference was our backgrounds. There were German Jews, Spanish Jews, French Jews - Jews from all over Europe were gathered there. My Romanian background set me apart. Perhaps my illness also contributed to my self-imposed isolation from the others. However, I did make a friend.

The elderly man in charge of the garden became fond of me, as well as impressed by my appreciation of his garden. He told me that I could come pick roses anytime I wished and take them home. I told him I didn't have a home, that I lived in the camp and that I would be in serious trouble if anyone found out about my visits. He kept my secret, and I enjoyed the roses in the garden, leaving them to be transported to Havana, the place where all of us in the camp longed to go.

The detainees at the camp included a large number of diamond cutters from Belgium who went on to establish a thriving business in Cuba during and after the war. From contacts we made in the camp, George later learned the skills involved in cutting and setting precious stones and worked in one of the diamond factories.

When more money arrived from the States and my father was able to pay the additional fees for entry into Cuba, we boarded a tender that chugged across the harbor to Havana.

Life in Havana

When we set foot on Havana's soil, there was help waiting for us. An organization called J.O.I.N.T., whose purpose was helping Jewish refugees settle, had an apartment for us. It was small with a balcony overlooking Old Havana. The streets were so narrow you had to press against building walls to allow a bus to pass. The streets were also dirty because the residents habitually threw their trash out the windows or over the wrought iron balconies of the Spanish-style buildings. While it was not the most desirable section of town to live in, the apartment was quite adequate, and we were once again free to live our lives, much like anyone else.

Soon we became familiar with our new home. To the west of the city's busy harbor was Old Havana. It's narrow streets were lined with stone houses with white tile roofs, while houses elsewhere in the city were more likely to be made of stucco. The most outstanding buildings were the Governor's palace, the cathedral, and a Dominican convent. But, my favorite spot was the Malecon, a popular promenade that extended along the ocean shore. The wide street and the splendid buildings that lined it rivaled Europe at its best.

We were, at last, in the capital of sugar, tobacco and rum, and my family's number one priority became learning Spanish. We accepted that it would become our family's language and set about in earnest to learn to speak it well. Spanish, being a romance language (akin to Romanian and French) was far less difficult for us than if we had faced the challenge of quickly learning German, Russian, English, Chinese or some other language with no root common to the two languages we already spoke.

Soon George and I began attending public school. I was originally placed in a grammar school because I spoke no Spanish; however, I learned the language in three months and was transferred to a high school. In Cuban history class, I learned details that have stuck with me ever since. For example, the early Spaniards intended building Cuba's capital on the southern coast, but that site proved too vulnerable to pirate attacks. In 1591, the Spaniards began to build Havana in a safer, yet often raided location. Among the invaders were British troops that captured and held Havana for almost a year in 1762.

At school, I met other girls from Europe. However, the three most important friends I made, I met when I joined an international Girl Scout troop. Fiona, Ingrid, and Jeanne became extremely close friends. Friends who remain in close contact with me to this day. After school, the four of us spent as much time together as possible. These were special friendships because we had so many common bonds. Two of us, Fiona and I, were from France; Jeanne and Ingrid were from Germany. We were all there, not because of something our parents or we had done. We were there simply as a result of having Jewish ancestors. Another bond was the need to quickly master Spanish.

Like me, my father also learned Spanish quickly and found a job with National Cash Register, a company with which he had had connections while in Europe. George also learned quickly. It was a slower process for our mother. It took fully six months before she spoke fluent Spanish. That's understandable because she spent much of her day alone, running the household, while people speaking Spanish surrounded the rest of us.

My father's European connections with National Cash Register Company must have been extremely strong, unless there was some Jewish connection, because anyone there on a visa could not legally work in the Cuban economy. You had to either find an employer who would agree to give you a job – without a work permit – start your own business, or work for another refugee who had started a new business that had been approved by the Cuban government. I am told that even those who started their own businesses were required to give at least half the jobs that they created to Cubans.

Whatever the arrangement, having mastered the local tongue, Papa began selling cash registers and became the Havana franchise's number one salesman. With that distinction came all the prizes and an excellent income. At that time, it was a status symbol in Cuba, as well as the U.S., for retail establishments to ring up their sales on an electric cash register. Continuing to use one of the old manually operated cash registers was a sign of not being successful. Therefore, my father had a wide open market; any retail establishment was a good prospect.

We had been in our Old Havana apartment less than a year when a terrible hurricane hit the city. The furious winds blew sheets of rain against the buildings, and water poured in from our balcony that faced the harbor. We mopped and mopped and mopped. Papa said he had no intention of our going through that ordeal again and told us we were moving.

By that time, he was doing fabulously well, so we packed and moved into an apartment in Vedado, the elite area of Havana and the location of the famous National Hotel. Our environment was instantly different.

Many of our neighbors were well-to-do refugees and wealthy middle class Cubans who were well educated and attended to cultural pursuits. We felt much more at home there. Our new apartment was large, very nice, and boasted a rear garden with a banana tree that kept us in ample supply of bananas. There we settled into what would be our normal life for some years to come. What pleased Mama the most was that for the first time since leaving Romania, we had a maid to come and clean.

The maid's name was Marta. She was a plump young woman with jet black eyes and ebony color hair, who always seemed to have a smile on her round face. Marta and my mother went shopping almost daily, and I occasionally went with them.

I still remember the smells of the market: the raw meat, the luscious fruits, the fresh vegetables, and the happy chaos of it all. While most of the Cubans lived on a diet that was dominated by beans and plantains, we often brought live lobsters back from the market and considered them a special treat.

One day, Marta had a pot of water boiling to cook the lobsters, and it was time for the tricky process of transferring the live creatures to the cooking pot. When my mother opened the bag that contained the lobsters, one escaped and went scurrying about the house. It was total pandemonium as Marta, my mother, and I chased the creature around the apartment, while we screamed, "*¡La langosta!*" Mama, who was wielding a broom, somehow managed to get the lobster onto the straw portion of the broom. She sped to the kitchen, shook the creature into the pot of boiling water, and slammed the lid onto it.

I think many of every person's memories involve food and drink. I'm no exception. I vividly recall the pungent aroma and strong taste of Cuban coffee. On the streets, you could buy a demitasse for one *quilito*, which was equivalent to a penny.

The Cuban ice cream was served in coconut shells, and street vendors used a special device to peel oranges and fresh pineapples for you. During the war, there was no rationing of sugar in Cuba; so, Hershey, which had a huge investment in Cuba, made certain we had a plentiful supply of chocolates.

The popular drink among my age group was *Materva,* a carbonated pineapple and orangeade. Coca-Cola was available; however, it was most often thought of as an essential ingredient in a *Cuba Libre*, a combination of Coke and the strong Cuban rum Añejo. While *Cuba Libres* were off limits to us youngsters, I do remember the wine.

Unlike in the United States, where wine is regarded as alcohol, in our household, as in most European cultures, wine was looked upon as a food and part of the meal. So, George and I were served wine at the table.

Of all the tropical fruits available to us, such as mangos, bananas, and pineapples, my favorite was *fruta bomba*, which translates bomb-shaped fruit.

(In the United States, we call it papaya. Because *papaya* is actually Cuban slang with a sexual connotation, we did not use that word in our home.)

Since Cuba was an agricultural country that survived primarily on the export of fresh produce, sugar, and rum, food was plentiful and available in great variety. Although we ate extremely well, our menus were quite different from any previous time in our lives.

Once again, we dressed well. Many of the Cuban women, who were highly adept at sewing, ran small seamstress shops. Our Cuban seamstress, Juanita, who was held in very high regard by my mother, made virtually everything Mama and I wore.

The move to a new neighborhood also meant I transferred to a better school, one a great many Europeans attended. Most of them were, like us, war refugees. At sixteen, my girlfriends and I, unlike most girls of that age in the States, were not allowed to date. We spent our days traveling about the city on our bicycles and riding to the beach together in search of a cool breeze.

Rose, 18, Havana, Cuba

To this day, I stay in close contact with several of these girlfriends and will tell more about them later. One of our common interests while in Cuba was our fascination with movies and movie stars. At that time, Ingrid Bergman was at her zenith as a star. She was my idol, the most beautiful and talented woman in the world, I thought. So, I wrote her a letter. In reply, she sent me an autographed picture. Years later, I had the opportunity of personally thanking her for it.

Despite our being in an environment in which we felt much more at home, safe and secure, my family did not socialize much, nor did many of the other refugees. In Cuba, when we got together with neighbors or business acquaintances, it was usually outside the home.

Over time, we found we had more Cuban friends than Jewish refugee friends because the Jewish colony there was not large. Also, the practicing Jews tended not to socialize outside their group.

Occasionally, we were invited to the French Embassy's functions. George and I looked forward to the Embassy's events, such as their celebration of Bastille Day each July 14th because there was a lot of food and wine and fun.

The grandest of the Embassy's celebrations came on August 25, 1944: the liberation of Paris. Champagne poured like water on that occasion. The only event that ever rivaled that party was on May 8, 1945 when all of Havana celebrated peace in Europe. The entire city became an unending street party.

Our family's inclusion in the French Embassy's festivities was prompted by my father's meeting with the French Consul General, Maurice Juster, in his unending efforts to get us into the United States. Because my father and Juster were both interested in chess, they became chess partners and good friends. Their mutual love of the game led to some social contact. Other than that, the major advantage for our family that came from their friendship was the Consul General's obtaining French passports for George and me.

After school each day, George worked part time in a diamond factory, where he learned to cut and set diamonds. Any job in the diamond factories was considered a blessing by any of the refugees because there were so many restrictions on employing anyone who was not a citizen of Cuba. Furthermore, the diamond factories paid well.

How these diamond factories came to Cuba is an interesting story in itself. After the U.S. entered the war, Congress passed a law saying that diamonds could no longer be cut for luxury purposes. They were needed in the war effort. The Jewish refugees from Antwerp, who had been in the diamond trade, went to the Cuban government and explained the opportunity. They had the skills and contacts to create an entirely new industry for Cuba, one with a ready market a short distance away in the United States. But, since refugees were not allowed to hold jobs in Cuba, the people skilled in cutting and setting the stones were unable to legally work.

The Cuban government decided that it was to its advantage to have a profitable new industry developed, one that would create jobs for skilled refugees and for unskilled Cubans. So, the diamond factories were established. At first, all were small; however, cutting and setting stones mined in Brazil quickly became Cuba's second largest industry, second only to sugar. Coffee moved down to third place, where it was being challenged by tourism.

1943

Hitler orders "scorched earth" policy and the Allies respond with round-the-clock bombing of Germany. The Eighth army reaches Tripoli, Russians destroy the German Army south of Stalingrad, and U.S. planes sink a 22-ship Japanese convoy in the Bismarck Sea. Mussolini falls from power as the allies invade Italy. General and Madame Chiang Kai-shek meet with Roosevelt and Churchill and agree to liberate Korea after the Japanese defeat. Americans were reading Betty Smith's *A Tree Grows in Brooklyn* and Georgia pilot Robert L. Scott Jr.'s *God is My Co-Pilot.* At the movies, Orson Welles' *Jane Eyre* and Alfred Hitchcock's *Shadow of a Doubt* score financial and critical success, while Rodgers and Hammerstein's *Oklahoma!* revolutionizes the Broadway musical. Penicillin, the jitterbug, rationing of meat, sugar, cheese, butter, canned goods, automobile tires, and shoes become a part of life in the U.S., while Cuba experiences none of the government-imposed shortages for those with money to buy.

First Job

After his graduation from high school in 1943, George began working full-time as a diamond setter, and I decided it was my turn to get a job. Many of the other girls my age had summer or part-time jobs to earn spending money, and I wanted to be among their ranks. So, I went downtown, looking for a possible position. I happened into a bookstore called *La Bohemia*, which was next to the Floridita Restaurant and its famous bar. The bookstore owner, whose name was Norman, was fully six feet tall, which is unusually tall for a Cuban. He was bald and had kind dark brown eyes. Norman quickly saw that I was well read, fluent in several languages, and genuinely interested in books. My knowledge of the authors represented on his shelves clearly impressed him; however, later he was to learn that my knowledge wasn't quite as broad as it might have seemed.

When I asked for a job, he said he thought it would be great having me work there. However, he was quick to point out that he paid very little. He was right about that. Still, the meager pay was enough to satisfy me, and I was hired on the spot.

Frequently, a disheveled old man walked in to browse through the books. He was dirty and smelly, but the shop's owner always treated him with great respect. I knew that this man usually came from the bar next door, and that was all I was interested in knowing about him.

One day when he dropped by, Norman was in the back of the shop. That seemed to please him. Instead of calling Norman to wait on him, while I scurried about fetching books for him, the man looked around with a smile and said in his fluent Spanish, "Rosita, climb up the ladder and get that last book on the top shelf for me."

The ladder he referred to was one of those that traveled on a track which ran the length of one of the walls of shelves. I knew what his game was because it wasn't the first time he had tried playing it. He wanted me to climb the ladder so that he could look up my skirt. As I made my ascent, I made certain to keep my skirt from flaring out.

When I caught him trying to sneak a look anyway, I dropped a book on his head. That made the dirty old man furious, and he stormed out of the shop, making more than enough noise to cause Norman to come out from his office to find out what was going on.

When I told Norman what had happened, he became as furious with me as the man who had just left did. "Don't you know who that man is?!!" he blustered. When I said that I didn't, Norman bellowed, "That's the world's most famous author. That's Ernest Hemingway!"

To me, he was still just a dirty old drunk who hung out at the Floridita Bar. (I later learned that he habitually had a breakfast there of raw egg with rum and a smelly Cuban cigar.) Norman told me that if I ever did anything like that again, he would fire me. But there was something about the way he said it that let me know he admired what I had done.

Hemingway did return, and I became the one busy elsewhere in the shop during his visits. On one occasion, I recall his coming in with a dashing young officer. After they left, Norman informed me that the young man was the author's son. It was many years later before I could admit to myself that, despite his personal habits and behavior, Hemingway was indeed a great writer.

1944

As World War II rages, the Arts thrive. T.S. Eliot publishes *Four Quartets*, John Van Druten's *I Remember Mama*, and Tennessee William's *The Glass Menagerie* triumph on Broadway, and Jean Giraudoux delivers his masterpiece *The Mad Woman of Chaillot* shortly before his death. Bartok completes his "Violin Concerto." Heavy air raids on London, D-Day landings in Normandy, June 6, the suicide of Rommel, the reelection of Franklin D. Roosevelt, the Allies capture of Orvieto and Cherbourg, make headlines along with U.S. bombing of Japan and crossing the German frontier. The Gold family and Havana's French colony celebrate the liberation of Paris, August 3rd.

My Suitors

Norman was my first – but undeclared – suitor. While he never made advances, nor did he say anything out of line, it was clear that he looked on me as more than an employee. The things he said and did not say told me he was considering me as a possible bride. He must have fallen in love with my brain because I was such a skinny child in those days, and I certainly had no interest in Norman. He was much older than I, no girl's idea of the dashing fellow who would one day sweep her off her feet.

After graduation from high school, at 17, I enrolled at the University of Havana. Dating without a chaperone was still considered out of the question by my family. Nonetheless, I soon had two very persistent suitors. I, however, was only interested in one of them, and the one who captured my interest most certainly was not Emil Grosswald.

Emil was a far cry from the ideal suitor the movies from the U.S. portrayed. He had skinny legs and arms, a big red nose, wore huge glasses with lenses that looked like the bottom of pickle jars and was in every way as physically unattractive as a man could be. I grant you he was brilliant; however, that's a deeper quality that seldom gets high ratings from a teenager. At the time, the only thing I could see that we had in common was our Romanian heritage. Aside from his total lack of physical appeal, he simply had no emotional control. For example, one day I was on a bus in Havana. Emil spotted me and began running after the bus, wildly waving his arms and screeching, "Rose! Rose! Rose!"

His comic scene was sufficient enough to stop the bus and, much to my annoyance, when he climbed on board, he took the seat next to mine. Emil was loud, his arms flailed about as he talked, and his adoration for me was embarrassing. I could hardly wait to get off the bus and flee his attentions.

Turning one cold shoulder after another didn't slow him one bit. Over and over Emil told my mother that he intended marrying me; however, he wanted to wait until I was older, since I was only seventeen and he was twelve years my senior. When he eventually learned that I was engaged, he gallantly ended his pursuit and gave me a set of towels as a wedding gift.

Many years later, I saw Emil again. By then, he had received his PhD. from the University of Pennsylvania and eventually went on to teach there. Emil was a mathematical genius, a kind man, and one haunted by the guilt of being a Holocaust survivor. Why he had survived when millions did not was an unfathomable question to him.

Perhaps the answer was to become the husband of Lissy Ronald. Lissy was a year younger than I and had also escaped to Havana; however, the two of us never met during our years there. But, she and Emil did meet, and the two kept in touch after they came to the United States. Eventually, he asked her to marry him. Much to Lissy's family's initial annoyance, she eloped with him to Saskatchewan where he had just acquired a position teaching. Leaving her life in New York behind, she became the wife of a mathematics professor. The couple soon moved to Philadelphia, and Emil became a highly regarded member of the faculty of the University of Pennsylvania.

It was during a trip to Philadelphia that I eventually met Lissy. She was lovely, completely dependent on Emil, and clearly adored him. He proved to be the person who could break through her deep depression and make her very happy. Theirs was as much a father-daughter relationship as it was a marriage, and she was terribly dependent on him for everything. This worked well for both, as long as he was alive; however, in 1989, after forty years together, Emil died at age 76. Not being willing to face life without him, Lissy committed suicide exactly one month after his death.

1945

The U.S. military enters Manila, Budapest falls, British troops reach the Rhine, while U.S. air raids on Tokyo, Cologne and Danzig succeed, and the war in Europe Draws to a close. The League of Nations holds its final meeting and turns over its assets to the United Nations, which forms the World Bank. Following the death of Franklin D. Roosevelt, Harry S. Truman is sworn in as President of the United States and learns of America's secret weapon, The Atomic Bomb. His decision to drop it on Hiroshima and Nagasaki brings war in the Pacific to an end. World War II casualties total 35 million, not including the 10 million who perished in concentration camps. The Nuremberg trials of Nazi war criminals begin, the Arab League is founded to oppose creation of a Jewish state, and Japan abolishes Shintoism. Frank Lloyd Wright's Guggenheim Museum design is unveiled; Mary Chase's invisible rabbit *Harvey* hops across the Broadway stage, and bebop comes into fashion. Vitamin A is synthesized, a B-25 bomber accidentally strikes the Empire State Building, and the Black Market thrives in Europe.

U. S. O. Holds Formal Dance Saturday At Hotel Nacional

A delightful dance was held last Saturday evening at the Hotel Nacional for the soldiers stationed at the U. S. Army Air Base at San Antonio de los Baños. It was sponsored by the U.S.O. in Havana, under the direction of Miss Barbara Beakes.

There were over two hundred in attendance; soldiers and their lovely partners dancing to the splendid music of Ramon Vidal and his Miramar Orchestra. A delightful buffet supper was served during the evening.

Many charming ladies from the prominent circles of Havana society, by their very presence and beautiful dancing made the party a great success. They were the following:

The Misses Mary Bussy, Carmen Bogardus, Pat Brussels, Betty Bryant, Nancy Bryant, Frances Beard, Jill Betancourt, Rosa Calderin, Maria Teresa Figueroa, Lolita Figueroa, Frances Folsom, Juliette Fischer, Esther Garcia, Rose Gold, Marjorie Harras, Mary Rosa Hillyer, Toto Henriquez.

Paulette Jallais, F. Justiz, Renée Katz, Vivian Kli, Mariana Leyva, Lolita Luis, Martha Lopez, Muriel Macy, Jeanette Makle, Harriet Margo, Olga Malkazits, Gilda Masvidal, Olga Morales, Dorothy Magoon, Mary Louis Mace, Geneva Nelson, Olga Ortiz, Delfina Perez.

Helen Rulison, Silvia Rodriguez, Elena Riveron, Mary Sisto, Cusa Sobredo, Maria Luisa Suarez, Jean Sgnanersta, Mary Stearns, Olga Torrens, Martha Torrens, Fabiola Villa, Esther Villa, Carmela Valdes, Magdalena Valdes and Marilyn West.

Hosts and hostesses for the evening were Mr. and Mrs. Gunther Harras, Mrs. John C. Margo, Mrs. Chandler Hill and Mr. Harry Manning.

Volunteer bar-tenders were Mr. H. B. Jeffre, Mr. Emil Schneider, Mr. Charles Lee, Mr. Harold Medeiros, Mr. Roger Johnson and Mr. Donald O'Keefe.

Newspaper account of Rose's "unforgettable" dance

John

At age eighteen, the suitor who caught my eye was an American. One of my girlfriends told me about the USO dances, which you could only attend if you had a chaperone. This appealed to me and even met with my mother's approval. Aside from the attraction of all those handsome men in uniform, the USO was a great place to dance.

I only attended one of those dances, but it was one I'll never forget. It was at that USO dance I met a young Air Corps lieutenant named John Cunningham. He was twenty-three, quite handsome and suave in his uniform. Although I couldn't speak much English and John spoke only English, we seemed to have little difficulty communicating. His mischievous, twinkling brown eyes did their own talking. It seemed he had danced with every girl there before he spotted me. I was clumsy and shy, but soon he whirled me in his strong arms and before I knew it, I was doing the jitterbug. Every remaining dance was with him, and as the final song of the night, "Let Me Call You Sweetheart" played, he held me too close for comfort and led me across the floor laughing at my great nervousness and excitement.

John began calling me, and somehow we managed to carry on phone conversations. He was stationed at Rancho Boyero Base, better known as Batista Field. The U.S. Air Force had leased it for the war effort, and there the Air Force trained B29 crews to make over-water flights. John flew airplane parts to the various training crews in Jamaica, Puerto Rico and the rest of the Caribbean area.

As our relationship progressed, there were also chaperoned picnics on the beach. During this time, I learned that he was a bombardier and had flown fifty combat missions in Europe. I also discovered that his commanding officer was the movie star Jimmy Stewart. John flew in B17's and B24's throughout the war. While stationed in San Pengrazio, Italy, he bombed Ploesti, the oil fields in Romania, as well as Bucharest, which was on the way to the oil fields. The bombs he dropped also shattered virtually every major city in Germany.

I wasn't the only one who was impressed by John; my mother liked him, too. In fact, she liked him enough to invite him to dinner. For the occasion, she and our Cuban maid, Marta, decided they wanted to impress my caller. They went through the time-consuming process of making the French fish soup bouillabaisse.

In the French tradition, my mother topped the guest of honor's soup plate with the head of the fish. When John looked into that fish's eyes, he literally turned green and had to leave the table. It was too much for the boy from Alabama. After he eventually returned to the table, the fish's head was out of sight in the kitchen.

In every respect, it was an awkward evening. In addition to the language barrier and John's embarrassment – as well as my mother's – over the fish head incident, there was my father's suspicious attitude toward John. Nonetheless, it was not the last I was to see of the lieutenant. John phoned frequently, and one day he called to ask me to meet him at the little café in front of the USO. Our verbal communication, by then, was good enough for me to understand that he wanted me to come on my bicycle, not with my mother.

When I got there, I noticed he was talking to a girl and avoiding me. Furthermore, he seemed very embarrassed. I took a seat at a table across the way and waited. When he eventually approached my table and sat down, I asked him who the girl was. He said he didn't know. In truth, he was embarrassed to tell me that it was one of the prostitutes who worked the area, and she was trying to interest John in her services.

It's strange the details we recall. For example, I remember that on that day, I had on a red knit sweater that had buttons shaped like question marks, and John asked me, "What were all those questions?" I coyly replied, "You will have to guess."

At one of our meetings, John told me he was being transferred back to the United States. After he left, we corresponded for a year. He wrote in English, and a friend of mine who spoke fluent English translated his letters for me, as well as my replies to John. During this time, John received his discharge from the Air Force and entered Georgia Tech to study architectural design. Eventually, one of his letters to me included a marriage proposal. It also proposed that we get married by proxy via the telephone. The basic idea was that we would marry by phone, which would give me war bride status. With that status, I could then travel to the United States to join John.

Beyond the usual resistance fathers have toward their daughters marrying, this proxy proposal did not sit well with my father. He headed to the U.S. Embassy to ask if such a thing was possible. The man with whom he talked said it was strictly illegal. When my father heard the word *illegal*, that triggered his suspicious nature, and he decided to hire a detective in the U.S. to investigate John. The detective uncovered some information that was news to me: John was married. This further angered my father, and he said that marriage to John was out of the question.

I called John to tell him what we had learned. When he heard my father had hired a detective to check him out, John was furious and told me, "I *was* married, yes. But I'm standing here with the divorce papers in my hand."

This changed my view to the point that I wanted to go ahead with the marriage. My father, knowing his headstrong daughter, said the marriage could take place. However, we had to respect his conditions. We could marry only if John returned to Cuba for the ceremony.

What the detective didn't uncover was that John's idea of a proxy marriage was strictly an economic decision. He had only his GI bill as income. In fact, in order to have enough money to get the two of us back to the U.S., John hitchhiked to Miami to take a Pan American flight to Cuba. At the time, unless you traveled by boat, there was no other option.

When he arrived, John presented himself to my father, told him that he loved me, and asked for my hand in marriage. He received my father's reluctant blessing because Papa clearly understood that I was determined to marry John and go to the United States. Absolutely determined.

My mother's apprehension focused on one thing John said to her when she, in a private conversation with him, raised the issue of my still being very young. John said that he wanted to marry someone young, a wife he could train, one he could mold to his way of thinking. To her that meant that, even after a yearlong courtship, John did not know me very well.

Nonetheless, after acquiring all the necessary papers and blood tests, on December 23, 1946, my parents, George, John and I headed for Havana's City Hall for the ceremony, which was completely in Spanish. When it came time for John to respond, I had to translate for him.

For the occasion, I wore a lovely light gray suit made for me by my seamstress and a beautiful corsage of rose buds that John gave me. From there, we went to the U.S. Embassy where I was classified as a war bride and

received a war bride visa. Then, we headed to a photographer to have our picture taken before proceeding to the Floridita Restaurant. I am happy to say Hemingway was not at his usual haunt on that particular night.

There we celebrated with an elegant dinner, and my parents presented us with a wedding gift of five hundred dollars. While that doesn't sound like a great deal today, at that time such a sum would more than pay for the lavish wedding celebrations that American debutantes expect today.

We spent our wedding night at my parents' home. The next day, we gathered our bags, which included my carefully packed trousseau of beautiful nightgowns and underwear that the seamstress had made for me. Later, when I unpacked the great quantity of the seamstress's handiwork, John looked at all the finery and asked, "Where are the clothes?"

In truth, the remainder of my wardrobe was slim in comparison to the amount of fancy lingerie. What I did have was ill suited for our destination's colder climate. In fact, I only had one coat, a light one that was more than ample for Cuba's mild winters.

Warm clothes or not, on Christmas Eve my parents saw us off on our flight to Miami. A final gift from my mother was a cooked turkey, which neither she nor I knew would be promptly confiscated because no meat could be taken into the U.S. Some immigration official's family must have had a grand Christmas dinner.

Part II

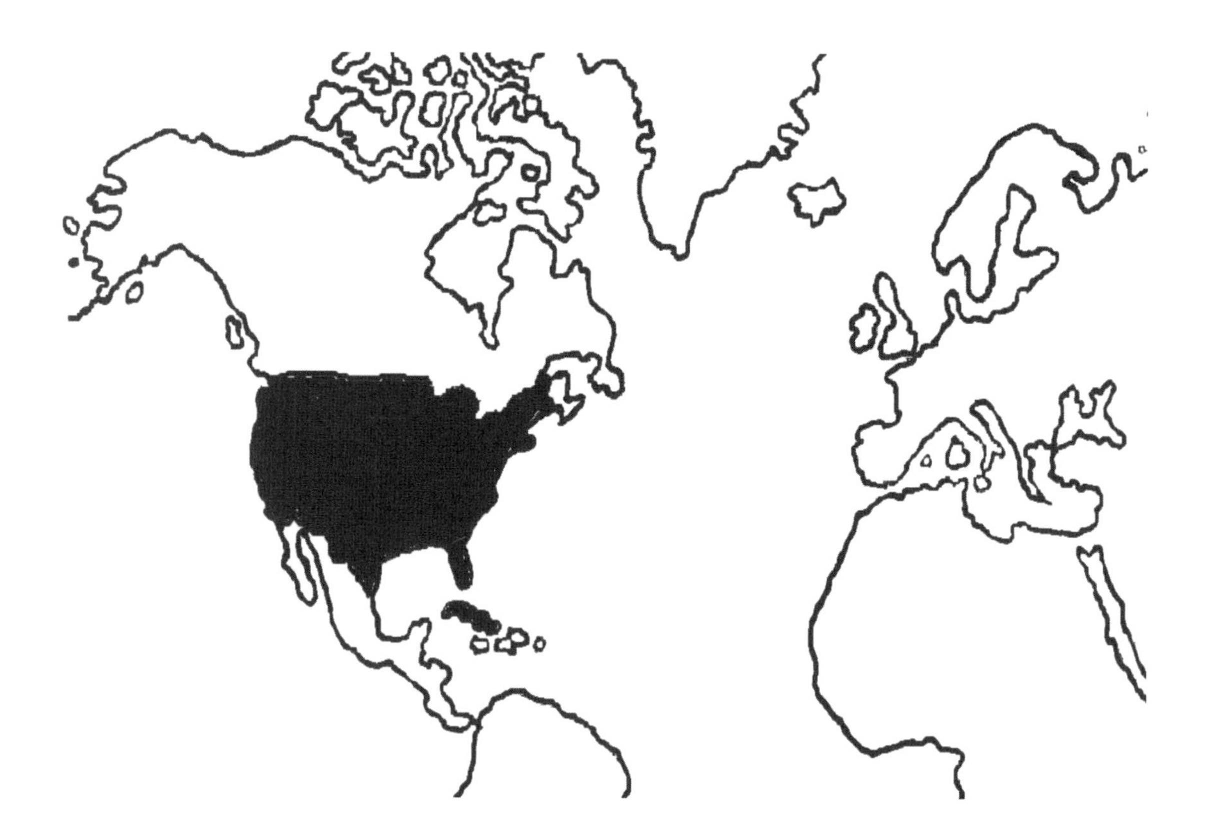

1947

After so many years of war, suspicions are slow to cede. WWII is technically over, but a "Cold" War between two newly anointed superpowers has begun. In defense against the threat of Communism, Harry Truman signs the National Security Act, which, in turn, creates the Department of Defense, the Joint Chiefs of Staff, the National Security Council, and the Central Intelligence Agency. Within a few months, these agencies target the movie & entertainment industry for refusal to co-operate with the House of Un-American Activities. In spite of the Cold War, many countries experience freedoms that they had never known: New Zealand and India both gain independence from the United Kingdom, and peace treaties are signed between the Allies, Italy, Hungary, Romania, and Bulgaria. In America, an angst-ridden Marlon Brando begs for "Stella!" in Williams' *Streetcar Named Desire*. Propaganda declines and wholesome entertainment reigns as Howdy Doody, *Miracle on 34th St.*, and the World Series are embraced by the country. Jackie Robinson and Chuck Yeager break the color line and the sound barrier. It is an exciting time to be in the U.S., and newlywed Rose Cunningham, neé Gold, experiences it all.

Welcome to the U.S.A.

On arrival at Miami's airport, U.S. immigration and I butted heads. The officials noticed on my passport that I was originally from Romania and demanded to know if I was a member of the Communist Party. I told them how old I was when we left and that the Communists were the reason that my family left Romania. That wasn't good enough to satisfy them, and they asked me scores of questions that my limited English could not handle. They brought in an interpreter to help me answer and the officer to understand. All this time, John was outside, not knowing what was happening. Finally, they stamped my passport, and I was, at last, on U.S. soil. To celebrate our arrival, John bought me my first hamburger.

There were surprises ahead, many of which severely tested my love for John and the wisdom of my choice. We did not transfer to another plane or even the train to reach Atlanta. We traveled by Greyhound bus. That long, tiring trip was twelve hours ... and seemed even longer. At least we didn't hitchhike. And, when we, at last, stepped off that bus, I couldn't believe how cold it was.

There were bigger and less pleasant surprises in store. I had no idea John was so poor. No assets. All he had was a one-door Jeep he had bought as war surplus. He had built a door for the passenger side. That addition was the full extent of the vehicle's creature comforts. In it, we headed for a private home in the Grant Park area where John had one room, a bath, and kitchen privileges.

From there, we went to John's family's home for Christmas dinner. His father, Charley, was a bus driver for Georgia Power Company, which then owned Atlanta's transit system of buses and trolleys. His mother's family was from Alabama and his father's from Georgia. In addition to his parents, John had two brothers and three sisters. At that time, they all still lived on the farm, which was their home. John was the oldest and the most educated, and had definitely acquired his polish at school and in the service. There had been another sister, the oldest, who married at seventeen. I later learned, her husband had killed her in a fit of jealousy. Of this group of five, only his mother, Edna, greeted me warmly. The rest were cold, distant, and uninterested in learning anything about me. They were all honest, decent people, but their fundamental religion and rural Southern background made them highly suspicious of me. I was a foreigner from multiple countries and Jewish. A

Jewess who had been reared Catholic and spoke little English was too much for them, a confusing threat.

After a period of concern and frustration over their reaction to and treatment of me, I realized that I didn't need these people. To this day, we've never been close and only see one another at funerals, which I admit is sad. Thanksgiving reunions at John's grandparents, in Alabama, formed the bulk of our contact.

There were others who were more friendly: his maternal grandparents, John and Edna, who, I found out, was one fourth Cherokee Indian and quite musical, and his Uncle Dub Hudgins, whom John was very fond of, because they went fishing and hunting together, creating a special bond.

Culture shock continued bombarding me from all sides. Along with my surprise, concerning the living conditions we faced, our visit to his grandparents' added another. John introduced me to something I'd never seen before: an outhouse. Furthermore, the temperature was a most unpleasant 20 degrees. Even in our humble Marseilles garret, we had indoor plumbing. Nothing seemed familiar: the weather, the people, or the customs. For example, in Havana, little was made of Christmas. There, Christmas was celebrated at the church. The big day for giving and receiving presents was the Twelfth Day of Christmas, Epiphany.

My initial reaction to the new world in which I found myself was fright. Nothing was familiar. John was the only person I really knew, and I admittedly didn't know him nearly as well as I had thought. There were many times when the urge to return to Cuba was great. However, I did not and applied myself to learning another language as rapidly as I could. Again, in three months, I had acquired another language - my fourth. I no longer had to point at items I wished to purchase.

There was a great deal more for me to learn. On one of my first solo city bus trips, I took a seat near the back of the bus. The driver saw what I had done, stopped the bus and came back to my seat to tell me I had to move up to the front. Only blacks sat in the back of the bus. This was my first exposure to segregation because there was no segregation in Cuba. Distinct class lines, yes. But, segregation, no. Fortunately, segregation was to soon become illegal throughout the U.S.

I also learned to drive, with John as my teacher and his beloved jeep at my mercy. At first, I seemed to have inherited my father's pathetic driving skills; however, I was determined to master that stubborn machine. And, I did.

About the time I was beginning to feel confident with my English, we moved to a house on McClendon Avenue, near Atlanta's Little Five Points, an old house, which had been divided into apartments. There, we had two rooms, a bath and kitchen. This would be our home for the next two years.

Shortly after the move, I felt I was ready to continue the college work that I had started at the University in Havana. I enrolled at Georgia State, taking classes in English, logic, philosophy, and drama. The latter led to my being in a play called *Oh, Henry!* In it, I played the role of a maid. At that time, my French/Spanish accent was so thick, I don't think anyone other than John understood a word I said.

I took three years of night classes at Georgia State; however, there was a break in my studies when John accepted a position with an architectural firm in Missouri. So, from the time I began college at the University of Havana, then at Georgia State, and finally at the University of Madrid, I covered the requirements for a degree in language arts.

While the GI Bill covered John's tuition costs, it did not cover mine. To pay my tuition costs, I got my first full-time job at the library on the Georgia Tech campus. That job didn't last quite a year. Simply put, the head librarian and I didn't get along well.

My next job was working at Atlanta Gas Light Company, as a clerk in the Addressograph Department. The equipment I operated would seem quaint and clumsy today, but then it was the state of the art way of addressing bills and other mass mailings to customers.

One payday, after I had been there about three months, a very distinguished man stopped by my desk and handed me a check. "Young lady, do you know who I am?" he asked. When I said that I didn't, he added, "I'm the person who signs your checks," and pointed out his signature on the face of the check. He was the vice president of finance, a Mr. Hattaway.

I looked him in the eye, as I turned the check over and asked, "Do you know who I am?" When he said that he didn't, I said, "I'm the person who signs the check on the other side."

With a hearty laugh, he took me by the hand and said, "You've got to meet the president," and took me to his office. While that made me better known in the higher echelons of the company, it didn't endear me to my fellow workers who viewed my response to Mr. Hattaway as arrogant and disrespectful. They missed the fact that he loved it. I guess they were very strata conscious and must have found company hierarchy somehow either uncomfortable or intimidating. I didn't, which is one of the reasons I've met and worked with so many power brokers and international figures over the years.

A year into our marriage, John and I were paid a visit by my parents. They came as tourists for their first glimpse of life in the United States. Our living conditions on McClendon and our lifestyle shocked them. Both John and I were in school and finances were a continual strain, and that was clearly evident to my parents. They made almost daily trips to the grocery store to bring home food.

My father, being the adventurous kind, discovered the Fulton Market, a place where vendors brought fresh produce and a variety of meats and fish. One day Papa returned from the market, proudly carrying a large carp. Mama was not at all happy about having to clean it, but she did. He bought the carp because someone had told him that it had caviar in it. But carp roe was nothing like the Russian caviar he had once enjoyed so much.

1949

Harry S. Truman is inaugurated President of the United States, the North Atlantic Treaty is signed in Washington, the Berlin blockade is officially lifted, and Israel is admitted to the U.N. The U.S.S.R. tests its first atomic bomb, and eleven U.S. Communists are found guilty of conspiracy to overthrow the government. William Faulkner is awarded the Nobel Prize for Literature and the curtain rises on a host of great plays, including T.S. Eliot's *The Cocktail Party*, Carson McCuller's *The Member of the Wedding*, and Rogers and Hammerstein's musical *South Pacific.* At the movies, *The Third Man* (which made zither music popular) and Jean Melville's *Les Enfants Terribles* become offbeat box office successes. The samba becomes the latest dance craze, while the most popular songs range from "I Love Those Dear Hearts and Gentle People" to "Rudolph the Red-Nosed Reindeer."

George

After two years on McClendon, we bought a house near Avondale Estates. The year was 1949. Since John was still in school, the GI Bill made the purchase possible. The little house was new, had two bedrooms and a large yard. I thought it was wonderful. In comparison to the two other places we had lived in Atlanta, it was a vast improvement. More importantly, it was ours. The price was eight thousand dollars, which did not include the cost of Amigo, the collie dog we also purchased.

My brother, George, soon occupied the new house's second bedroom. He came to Atlanta on a student visa to study English at Georgia State and stayed with us for nearly two years. I absolutely rejoiced over George's arrival. He was family and my tie to the past. George had a fantastic sense of humor and brought a great deal of joy to the household.

One Sunday, he went to a Baptist church that made a point of welcoming foreign visitors. There he met a girl named Erma, who was the daughter of missionaries. They had taken her to West Africa when she was a small child. Her religious beliefs were quite different from my brother's blend of Roman Catholic and Jewish theology. Nonetheless, George and Erma were attracted to one another. It was a case of opposite attraction. George was definitely exciting, out-going, witty and nice looking. Although, Erma was a good person and fairly attractive, she was not someone you would call exciting.

When George had to return to Cuba to take care of legal papers, Erma, much against her parents' wishes, went with him and met my parents. She and my mother got along quite well. My father, however, was another matter. It seemed nothing Erma said, thought, or did was to his liking. This didn't seem to matter to either her or George, and on their return to Atlanta, they began making plans for a big, church wedding. My parents came over for the occasion, still not thrilled about George's choice of a bride.

The newlyweds got their own house, and within a year, their first child was born. George decided that he needed a job that would pay well. Since there were no jobs available for gem cutters or setters, he looked toward a field that interested him greatly: food and wine. Even though he had never formally studied either, on his own, he had become highly knowledgeable about both.

After applying at several restaurants in town, he landed a job at Atlanta's most prestigious private establishment, the Piedmont Driving Club. There he was in charge of wines. Management and members liked him, and he eventually became the club's assistant manager.

George stayed at the Driving Club for nearly six years. His pleasant personality made him well liked, and women adored him. This latter quality didn't help the marriage. Like father, like son - he became a womanizer, eyes forever wandering.

To balance the favor of providing a member of my family with a temporary home, we later invited John's sister, Mary, to stay with us for a couple of years. Unfortunately, she and I did not get along nearly as well as John and George did.

Later in his life, while George was managing the Holiday Inn in Gatlinburg, Tennessee, he became ill. In 2000, he died of Alzheimer's disease. I miss this special man and think of him every day.

Citizenship

Shortly after George's wedding, I had been in the U.S. the required two years for women with "war bride" status to apply for U.S. citizenship. To prepare for the test, I began a crash course of my own design on U.S. history and governmental structure.

When it came time to take my exam, I almost missed the simplest question. The man administering the test asked me to describe the American flag. Instead of my saying it had thirteen stripes and forty-eight stars, I transposed the numbers. He stared at me and asked, "Young lady, have you ever looked at an American flag?"

I quickly corrected myself and passed the examination.

The citizenship ceremony was quite impressive to me. I, along with half a dozen European girls and some Orientals stood in a row in our knee-length dresses and hats to take the oath. We were all war brides. The press was there to take our picture for the next day's paper, and I was the one the reporter chose to interview for the accompanying article.

Citizenship for War brides, 1949. Rose is third from the left.

In connection with becoming a citizen of the United States, the occurrence that stands out most vividly in my mind was being told that I could not retain my French citizenship. In those days, unlike today, a dual citizenship was not allowed. I didn't think twice about my decision. I was most willing to give up my French citizenship because I was extremely proud of becoming an American citizen.

I admired and appreciated the opportunities here and the abundance of freedom I had never experienced before: freedom of speech, freedom of religion, freedom to become the best that one could be. I saw that if you really worked, you could get somewhere, and I was deeply grateful for the opportunities before me.

One reason I was so anxious to become an American citizen as quickly as possible was to be able to help my parents get out of Cuba. Knowing all too well the devastating results of Communism in Romania, we could see the handwriting on the wall. Cuba's corrupt government was making Communism's utopian promises seem very appealing to the general population. Clearly the overthrow of Batista's government was only a matter of time. The day after I became a citizen, I went to fill out all the documents necessary to get my parents into the U.S. permanently.

At that time, if you had a relative who was a U.S. citizen, the volume of red tape and paperwork for a visa was a mere fraction of what you had to deal with if you did not have immediate family ties in the U.S. My citizenship got them top priority status on the list. Within a year, they had their visas, packed and moved to Atlanta.

The positive side of this for both was they were able to live in the United States and in the same city as their children. The negative side was their having to start all over again, making new friends and learning a new language. They both enrolled in night school. Within about five months for my father and about six for my mother, both were fluent in English.

On their arrival in the U.S., my parents lived with John and me in our little house in Avondale Estates. As wonderful as it was having Mama and Papa with us, the house was far too small, and John and Papa were never meant to live under the same roof.

After six months, my parents purchased a house not far from us in Avondale. Still, that did not suit Papa. He hated it there because the neighborhood had no sidewalks, and he was an avid walker. He considered not placing the comfort and convenience of walkers above all else barbaric. Later, after John and I moved to the house we still call home, Mama and Papa sold their house and chose to live on Peachtree Street at the Howell House, a prestigious address at the time.

In that neighborhood, he had miles of sidewalks and Piedmont Park nearby. He could walk till his heart was content.

Later, in 1979, this proximity to the park, teamed with Papa's libido, incubated a situation that was exasperating at the time - funny in retrospect. I received an urgent call from my distraught mother, saying she had just received a call from the police station. "Your father has had a heart attack," she wailed, "Please go!"

A heart attack? At the police station? It didn't make sense. I called the police and was told, "Yes, Mr. Gold is here, but he didn't have a heart attack. We arrested him for creating a disturbance."

At the station, I found my father in perfect health, with the exception of a bruised dignity. He regally waited there, dressed in Bermuda shorts, knee length socks, white shoes, a French beret, and holding an elegant walking stick.

According to the police – and I have no reason to doubt them – he was strolling through the Piedmont Arts Festival when he spied a gorgeous, scantily dressed woman. Papa approached and pinched her.

When he did, he bargained for trouble he hadn't anticipated. The woman was an undercover police decoy placed there to apprehend drug peddlers. Instead, she apprehended Papa for making a pass at her and took him to the station in a police wagon. At the station, she found herself the laughing stock of the police force for apprehending an 85-year-old, horny Frenchman.

After I paid his twenty-dollar fine, Papa stormed out of the police station exclaiming, "Barbarians! In France they would have decorated me."

After Papa mastered English, he became a salesman for a company that made office equipment. He could sell anything and proved, again, to be an excellent salesman.

Because we were so close, my parents' social life became limited to our family and my circle of friends. The fact that neither of them drove didn't help matters. Consequently, Mama and Papa had little contact with people their own age.

Outside of work, my father did not make friends as readily as Mama. In fact, he could be decidedly unfriendly. His relationship with my brother was a prime example. There was always animosity between Papa and George, which prevented the two of them from ever being close. Papa belittled George, even as an adult, which was very unfair.

On the other hand, I was our father's pride and joy, faultless in his eyes. His blindness towards George's strong points and accomplishments – and perhaps towards my faults – saddened my mother. However, she was resigned to Papa never treating either of us in a fair, balanced manner.

1950

Britain recognizes Communist China, there are riots in Johannesburg against apartheid, Truman instructs the U.S. Atomic Energy Commission to develop a hydrogen bomb, the U.N. Building is completed, and paranoid Senator Joseph McCarthy advises Truman that the State Department is packed with Communists. King Leopold III returns to Belgium after six years in exile, and King Gustavus V of Sweden is succeeded by his son Gustavus VI. Ray Bradbury raises science fiction to an art form with *The Martian Chronicles*, and Hemingway publishes *Across the River and Into the Trees.* Benny Goodman premiers Aaron Copeland's "Clarinet Concerto", Abe Burrow's *Guys and Dolls* and Giancarlo Menotti's *The Consul* are the talk of the musical stage, while black singers Nat King Cole and Eartha Kitt share the pop music spot light with folk singers' renditions of songs from Israel, "Good Night, Irene" and "Tzena, Tzena." Antihistamines are introduced to allergy sufferers, 30,000 varieties of roses are catalogued, and movies *All About Eve* and *Sunset Boulevard* not only win Academy Awards, they are winners at the box office, as well.

Life in St. Louis

Shortly after my parents' arrival and completing their English courses, John graduated from Georgia Tech. The school also awarded me a diploma: "Mistress of Patience in Husband Engineering."

Following graduation, he was offered an excellent job with Bank Building and Equipment Corporation, a company based in St. Louis that specialized in the design and construction of banks. While the company had an Atlanta office, they wanted John to go to St. Louis. So, we packed our bags, rented our house, and took a train to St. Louis.

We settled into an apartment, and I got a clerical job at a government agency. I have little more than three pleasant memories of St. Louis. One was Sticks Department Store. It was a wonderful place to shop. Another was the cheesecake you could get in that town. Delicious! And, the third was St. Louis' famous zoo. We lived near it, as well as near the Mississippi River. During our year-and-a-half there, we experienced the most miserable summer and freezing winter either of us have ever known. Horrendous heat. Insufferable cold, cold enough for the river to freeze over. The ice was so thick we found we could skate on it. The town was very German, which also did not endear it to me.

To qualify for my government clerical job, I had to take a typing test, which turned into a comedy of errors. While I am and, at the time, was a good typist, tests rattle me. To make matters worse, they seated me in a low chair at a high table. I looked around and saw some telephone books. When I placed a very thick one on my chair, it over compensated and placed me up too high. So, I placed a thinner book under the typewriter. Now I was ready. The woman administering the test said, "Go," and I typed my fastest. When I hit the return lever on the manual typewriter I was using, the typewriter sailed off its phonebook and hit the floor. They gave me a second try on another typewriter that was in another area of the office, and I did pass – but just barely. The important thing to me was the job was mine.

After a year and a half, John and I admitted to one another that we had no desire to make St. Louis our home. There was little about the place that appealed to either of us, and the idea of another winter there was not acceptable.

We also saw that John's possibilities for advancement in St. Louis were not attractive enough to keep us there. I must admit, however, that he gained valuable experience designing banks for the firm. In fact, it steered him towards specializing in banks, and during our 56 years together, he has designed 186 bank buildings, as well as 30 jails, and numerous other commercial structures. John is also a published author, an accomplished sailor, and a part-time farmer.

John bought a new car with some of his earnings and resigned from his position. We packed our new Ford with our belongings and headed for Atlanta. It would be our home. On our return, he applied at an Atlanta architectural firm, Abreu and Robeson, and accepted the job offer he received.

Unfortunately, John did not know that the firm was in great financial trouble when he accepted the offer. He soon found himself unemployed. When he got the news, he told me that he thought the best thing for him to do was go into business for himself. And that's what he did.

1956

U.N. attempts at peace in the Middle East flounder. Khrushchev denounces Stalin's policy, Nasser, newly elected President of Egypt, attempts seizure of Suez Canal, but U.N. intervenes. Soviet troops march into Hungary, Japan is admitted to the U.N., Martin Luther King emerges as leader of U.S. campaign for desegregation, and Fidel Castro lands in Cuba with a small-armed force, intent on the overthrow of dictator Fulgencio Batista. John K. Kennedy wins Pulitzer Prize for *Profiles in Courage*, the drama *The Diary of Anne Frank* also wins a Pulitzer. Bernard Buffet and Jackson Pollock become the new finds in the art world, and big screen epics *Around the World in 80 Days, The Ten Commandments,* and *Lust for Life* dominate movie screens. Broadway falls in love with *My Fair Lady*, while Maria Callas and Elvis Presley stun the world with their vocal and personal styles. Transatlantic telephone service is inaugurated, Albert Sabin develops an oral polio vaccine, and Soviet athletes are the stars of the Olympic Games in Melbourne.

John's Career Path

Initially design assignments were sparse. John augmented our income from his practice by becoming proficient at delineations. In those pre-computer graphics days, in order to add color to a rendering of a building, the standard method was hand tinting with watercolors. Major buildings were sometimes even painted in oils. Whatever the color medium, the process was slow and tedious.

Airbrush painting offered a faster method with a new look that was appealing to architects and their clients. So, John became the master of the airbrush, while I called on all the architects in town to sell his services. I got to know many of Atlanta's powerbrokers on my sales trips, including a classmate of John's, architect John Portman.

In addition to being John's sales representative for delineations, I took a job at Scripto, an Atlanta-based firm that was one of the pioneers in the production of ballpoint pens. I also resumed taking night classes at Georgia State.

John had designed a house for us, one that was contemporary, contained space for an office and the family we planned to have – even a future maid's room. The office would be on the ground floor, with a separate entrance. Through the GI Bill, he acquired financing and construction began. He worked out of our house's office to get his first bank projects.

Steadily John's firm grew and he formed a partnership with another architect, an Englishman named Bill Burroughs. They moved the firm from the ground floor of our house to an old house they rented. It was off Piedmont Road, and today, the land is part of the Lindbergh Marta complex.

The partnership with Burroughs did not last long, but John's business thrived. Soon, he needed larger and better quarters, and he was tired of paying rent. A house on Cheshire Bridge Road was purchased, one that provided the space needed for growth. After moving to this location, John formed a partnership with Roy Forehand.

At their zenith, they had 20 employees and a thriving design firm that specialized in banks, courthouses, and other municipal buildings. Today that Cheshire Bridge location still stands and is home to a cooking school, where I recently took classes from an accomplished German chef who taught me how to cut an onion without crying.

Not only did the new partnership gain a reputation as specialists in the design of banks, courthouses and other municipal buildings, but John also became interested in banks - how they operated, and what made one successful.

His studies lead to the organization of First National Bank of Tucker, where he was elected Chairman of the Board. After a year, John resigned this position because it took him away from what he enjoyed most: architectural design.

1957

The Eisenhower Doctrine is formulated for protection of Middle Eastern nations from communist aggression, The International Atomic Energy Agency is established, Israeli forces withdraw from Sinai Peninsula and hand over Gaza Strip to UN forces, and the UN reopens the Suez Canal. The U.S. resumes aid to Israel, King Hussein proclaims martial law in Jordan, and Harold Macmillan succeeds Anthony Eden as Great Britain's Prime Minister. Eugene O'Neill's *Long Days Journey into Night* wins him a posthumous Pulitzer, and *The Bridge on the River Kwai* wins an Oscar, while Bernstein's *West Side Story* and Meredith Wilson's *The Music Man* illuminate Broadway. 13 year-old Bobby Fischer becomes chess champion, the Cha Cha Cha is the dance craze, "Chanson d' Amour," along with novelty tunes "The Purple People Eater" and "The Chipmunk Song" become U.S. favorites. Dr. Seuss introduces the world to *The Cat in the* Hat, and John and I introduce the world to our first daughter Valerie.

Becoming Parents

While John was busy building his business and building our house, we were also busy building a family. In fact, we moved into the new house only six weeks after the birth of our first child, Valerie.

It proved very difficult for me to become pregnant. We went to seek the help of Dr. Velkoff, who was Atlanta's only invitro fertilization specialist in 1956. With his help, we reached our goal. I became pregnant and was thrilled over the prospects of becoming a mother.

But, I was absolutely terrified by the notion of enduring the birth process. Consequently, when it was time to head for the hospital, I decided that the only way to calm myself was to drink something before reaching the delivery room. Just before we headed out the door, I downed a quarter of a bottle of cognac.

I'm well aware that, today, drinking any alcohol during pregnancy is considered unwise and dangerous; however, if you consult the medical journals of the time, you'll discover a great many articles by respected physicians who advocated moderate alcohol consumption during pregnancy.

What I did, however, was not remotely moderate. By the time John got me to Georgia Baptist Hospital, I was not only drunk - for the first time in my life - but, the alcohol had stopped the labor process, which meant they had to induce labor.

It goes without saying that the staff of a Baptist hospital was shocked to see me in the inebriated state in which I arrived. Despite all this, the following day, a very cold January 12, 1957, I delivered Valerie, my first child.

The alcohol issue didn't end there. When my mother arrived at the hospital, she was appalled to learn that wine was not served to patients with their meals and told Dr. Velkoff so. Nonetheless, the hospital was not moved to change its policies ... nor was Mama moved to change her opinions.

While I was a very immature mother, one who knew nothing about the care of an infant, John, on the other hand, was extremely knowledgeable. He had grown up the oldest in a large family, and he took over. He knew what a baby needs and how to deal with every circumstance that came along. The older I become, the more appreciative I am of his knowledge and help.

1959

Batista flees Cuba, Fidel Castro becomes Premier and expropriates U.S.-owned sugar mills. Belgium grants reforms in the Congo, DeGaulle is proclaimed President of the Fifth Republic in France, anti-Semitism flares at Cologne, Germany, and Hawaii becomes 50th state of the U.S. Norman Mailer publishes *Advertisements for Myself*, Vance Packard writes *The Status Seekers*, and *The Miracle Worker* plays to standing room only. The first U.S. nuclear-powered merchant vessel, "Savannah" is launched, U.S.S.R. Lunik reaches the moon, U.S. Postmaster General bans D.H. Lawrence's *Lady Chatterley's Lover* from being mailed on grounds of obscenity, and World Refugee Year is proclaimed. Film hits are diverse: *Anatomy of a Murder, Our Man in Havana, Hiroshima Mon Amour, Ben Hur, and La Dolce Vita.* Popular songs are equally diverse: "Mack the Knife," "Tom Dooley," "Everything's Coming up Roses," and "Personality." And, our second daughter is born and named Marcelle in honor of my father, Marcel.

Motherhood

Following Valerie's birth, our attempts at enlarging our family didn't go well, and I experienced two miscarriages. But, success did follow. On July 10, 1959, Marcelle was born. For her delivery, I assure you I was totally sober. Also, I was much better prepared to care for an infant, thanks to all I had learned from John.

One of my regrets is that we didn't have more children. I'm not certain I would have voiced that sentiment when I had one toddler tugging at my skirt and an infant in my arms. In retrospect, however, I deeply regret not having more children and would love being surrounded by a large family.

I believe I was a good mother, even though I was not the one hundred percent maternal type who gives up everything else in her life for her children. I tried to balance motherhood and its responsibilities with other interests in my life. Motherhood did not stop me from developing my languages or from involvement in social activities. For example, when our daughters were in grammar school, I took Italian lessons from their piano teacher and studied on my own until I had added a fifth language to the list of those I speak. I enjoyed it all, and think my career experiences helped me contribute more to the development of Valerie's and Marcelle's lives than John did. He was the disciplinarian in our family, and I still think he was too harsh and demanding. Duty and responsibility were the issues he focused on, while travel and experiencing the world were my focus. I took the girls everywhere from the opera and museums to festivals and movies. They didn't miss out. Consequently, I think I introduced them to the excitement of life and helped our girls develop a taste for things that were beyond the ordinary.

It should be no surprise that I made certain they spoke more than one language. I remember that their Spanish was good enough to get them on a television show for Spanish speaking children. At home Valerie, Marcelle and I spoke English with John, French with my father and mother, and some Romanian with my mother, and we spoke Spanish with Zeneida, our petite, middle-aged, dark-skinned, black-eyed live-in maid from Costa Rica. It was not a typical childhood for them, and of that I'm quite pleased.

Both children started their education at an exceptional preschool, Emory University's Arlington Academy. Later, they attended Kittridge and Briarcliff High. With John, they attended church at St. Andrews Presbyterian Church, where he was an elder, as well as the architect of the building.

Perhaps, this is the appropriate place to insert my religious beliefs. Earlier I wrote about my childhood fascination with the pomp and ceremony of Roman Catholicism. That was before I got a close-up look at organized religion in action. As a teenager, the more I learned about the horrors of war, the Vatican's indifference towards the suffering of the Jews, and the inhumanity that people who profess to be religious inflict on others with different beliefs, my fascination with Catholicism and religion in general became sorely tested. Over time, I reached a point where I no longer even believed in a supreme being. Later, however, I turned away from atheism and returned to my belief in God.

While I am very spiritual, I don't feel a need for involvement in organized religion to assert my belief. I find God in nature and don't need the church environment and weekly preaching. In fact, I have a limited tolerance for it. I have seen how it can dominate your life and rob you of your individuality. Some people seem to need that dominance, and that's fine for them. As for me, I don't need it. So, our girls' religious instruction fell to John.

When Valerie and Marcelle were approaching their teens, they learned to ride, went to horse shows, and attended a summer camp for girls, Camp Tonawanda, which was in the mountains of North Carolina. Camp was a good experience for them. There they learned to swim well and enjoy the full range of activities and the friendships that are all part of the summer camp experience. Camp gave them another outside world contact that they would not have otherwise experienced.

My parents were constantly in their lives. They came to our house every weekend and were a part of whatever activities we were involved in, both social and cultural. My parents even rented a summer cottage in North Carolina, in order to be near our girls while they were at camp. This bond between the children and their grandparents was important to me, and I believe it was to all of them. Unfortunately for all, the girls were never close to John's family.

During their high school years, both our girls and I became involved with student exchange programs. Marcelle spent a summer in France, and Valerie spent a summer in Costa Rica with the family that headed Coca-Cola operations there. In return, their daughter Ingrid visited us during their major school break, which took place during the holiday season, instead of summer.

Later at age 15, Valerie went to a private school in Vevey, Switzerland for a year in order to learn to speak fluent French. In truth, education was not the sole reason for sending her there, and at first, she did not want to go and leave her friends at Briarcliff High. Furthermore, we didn't want to be separated from our daughter; however, her new circle of Atlanta friends disturbed us because some of them were into drugs. Switzerland became the more attractive of the two alternatives.

From the school in Switzerland, she went to Berry Academy in Rome, Georgia. As a youngster, John had attended Berry Academy and then continued his education at Berry College, completing one year before entering military service. He knew the school well and that its emphasis was on work and study ethic. The values taught there and the school's high academic standing were an excellent choice for Valerie, the right place for her to complete her high school education. Temporarily, her education stopped there because she decided marriage was the next step for her.

Marcelle was quite athletic, a cheerleader, involved in tennis and track. Her high school accomplishments filled her room with trophies. She loved to ride and she had her own mount, a chestnut colored quarter horse named J.J. After graduation, Marcelle attended North Georgia College in Dahlonega, Georgia, and then she acquired her MBA from Imede, an exclusive business school in Lausanne, Switzerland, which is an extension of Harvard University.

While the girls traveled with us much of the time, I often traveled alone. I persuaded John to go with me to Europe and make the trip by ocean liner. The girls stayed with John's uncle Dub Hudgins in Alabama. I really liked that man. He appeared, at first, to be a redneck and a macho womanizer, but when you got to know him, you realized you were talking to a highly intelligent person. By the time we returned, both of our girls had heavy southern accents. As he had with John, Dub taught the girls to fish and enjoy the outdoors. While the children were working on their Alabama accents, John and I toured Italy, Greece, Israel and France. We crossed over on the S.S. United States, the only stainless steel ocean liner. It made the trip in five days, instead of the usual seven.

My Parents

John loved my mother's company but merely tolerated my father. The feeling was mutual; Mama loved John, but Papa most certainly did not. The two men were total opposites. Nonetheless, we took trips as a family, and I would go pick my parents up for their weekend stays with us. Papa refused to drive after the War, and my mother never learned to drive; so, in essence, I became their chauffeur, with a bit of help from the taxi companies and Atlanta's system of buses and trains.

Following my mother's death in 1989, we placed Papa in a North Carolina nursing home. It was George's turn now to see to Papa's needs, and since George was living nearby in Sylva, he was able to check on our father frequently.

Papa seemed happy enough there, and George and I thought things were going well. However, about a year after Papa was moved to the nursing home, I received a call from the head of the facility. She was highly agitated by my father's behavior and reeled off a string of instances in which Papa had upset the nurses with his sexual innuendoes and passes. During that call, I was told that she, the head nurse, and the remainder of the staff had decided that his behavior was abnormal and were convinced he should be committed to a mental institution. While I didn't agree and told her so, George and I finally did submit for Papa to be transferred to a hospital for testing. There would be no peace or quiet until he was thoroughly examined by a certified psychologist and had undergone two weeks of observation.

Following the two weeks of close scrutiny, he had to go before a judge who had the power to commit him or set him free. When the judge saw the charges, he said, "You bring me a 94-year-old horny Frenchman and want me to believe he's crazy? I can only hope that, if I reach his age, I'll be equally crazy."

With that, Papa was sent back to the nursing home. And, there he stayed for the remainder of his life. Up until the end, at age 97, he was an avid reader who was highly interested in international affairs and the world around him. I think his unending quest for knowledge was one of the reasons his mind stayed clear and alert and also contributed to his long and active life.

1960

Though the U.S. Supreme Court upholds that Louisiana's anti-integration laws are unconstitutional, South Africa's struggle against Apartheid takes a heavy blow when Afrikaner police open fire on unarmed demonstrators, killing 69 and injuring 180. Women come into the spotlight when the Food and Drug Administration approve the sale of the birth control pill in America, Sri Lanka elects Sirimavo Bandaranaike as their Prime Minister, making her the world's first female head of government. Stanley Kubrick and Alfred Hitchcock challenge social mores about sensuality versus sexuality and madness versus murder in *Spartacus* and *Psycho*. While America is alternately being horrified and entertained, the government announces its intention to send 3500 troops to Vietnam. That same government is overturned later in the year by the narrow victory of John F. Kennedy over Richard M. Nixon. Eisenhower's previous staff had helped in the resettlement of Cuban refugees, and by the beginning of Kennedy's term, there are 1,000+ Cubans arriving in the southeast per week. The amount of Spanish-speaking peoples in America doubled within three months.

International Activity Begins

While I enjoyed being a mother, parenthood didn't give me the sense of accomplishment that I needed or the international contacts that I craved. A partial answer to my needs came in the form of a small group called The International Club of Atlanta. Atlanta did not have a large cosmopolitan population at that time, and not many of the foreigners living here were involved in the organization. But that soon changed, and a large part of that growth was due to my involvement.

I held various offices in the organization and introduced many people to the club and its activities. It became a highly social group that frequently held parties and international fairs. Our common bond was our European or Oriental backgrounds and the fact that we thought on a different level: a level that embraced more than local issues and church involvement. It was a social as well as a religious tie that long-established Atlantans shared. While there is nothing wrong with such a bond, it didn't appeal to me at all. The club, however, did.

The International Club of Atlanta grew until its size became a problem. Therefore, the organization evolved into a number of more specialized groups, each with its own geographic entity. There was a French club, a German club, a Swiss club, and so forth. For example, when the Spanish club, known as The Spanish Circle (*Circulo Hispano)*, was formed, I focused my attention on it and served as its president. Initially, the club met at my house. We held an annual fair for the general public and many parties for the members. Today, I've been told, there are more than 50 of these clubs meeting in the Atlanta area.

Eventually, my position as an honorary consul and my involvement with the Atlanta Chamber of Commerce opened doors for all of these clubs. I was able to give them assistance in attaining higher profiles and tackling more ambitious projects that have helped Atlanta become a much more international city.

My initial involvement with the International Club of Atlanta still was not enough to fill my need to be involved in the local scene and experience accomplishment. John had pulled himself up by his bootstraps and had a right to be proud of his success. I wanted the same satisfaction.

Seeing no appealing opportunities, I decided it was up to me to create my own, find my own way of making a contribution and, at the same time, create within myself a sense of accomplishment. So, I went to the YMCA and asked if they had ever considered offering Spanish and French conversation classes for adults in the evenings. The idea appealed to them, and I was asked to make a proposal.

What I offered was eight weekly evening classes per course. When they heard this, they said that their only concern was textbooks. I told them not to worry about that; I would write my own. And I did. My initial text has been refined over the years and has become the standard text for all of Emory University's non-credit Spanish conversation classes.

The YMCA night classes proved quite popular and expanded to include French classes, as well as Spanish. Teaching filled a great need for me. I was making money and meeting interesting people.

Grant

Among the students who attended my Spanish classes was a man I'll call Grant. He was a handsome, muscular man with dark brown hair and eyes that showed his intelligence and social polish. He already spoke Spanish but needed the opportunity to practice it to better prepare himself for business dealings in Hispanic countries. While that's certainly no problem in the Atlanta of today, it was at that time.

After one of the classes, a couple of the other students came to me and asked if I knew who this man was. When I shrugged and said that I didn't, they told me he was one of the richest men in Atlanta. To me, he was simply one of my students. What mattered most was his eagerness to learn.

One day Grant asked if I'd teach him privately. I said that I would; however, the classes would have to be at my house. He was agreeable with that, we settled on a fee, and the private classes began.

For months, I tutored Grant without having an inkling of what was going on in his mind because he worked hard on mastering Spanish. Then, the truth came out; Grant was in love with me. During a tutoring session, he put his hand on mine and made his confession. When he did, I was dumbfounded and didn't have the experience to know how to react – but I was most certainly intrigued.

Once he mustered the courage to tell me about his feelings for me, the man was nothing less than persistent. Each day there was a letter from him, a letter in Spanish. As busy as this man was, he took the time to write a daily letter by hand in his beautiful and precise script. On the rare occasions when there was no mail, he would call.

We exchanged numerous philosophical ideas. In letters, we described our philosophies about life in general. For example, we often quoted from Lin Yutang's "Wisdom of Confucius" - an immortal Chinese sage whose ideas are as vital today as they were 2500 years ago. We discussed theological thoughts on such writing as "The Kingdom of God is truly within the man himself" and Confucius' "Respect the heavenly and earthly spirits and keep them at a distance."

We exchanged ideas on the writings of Dr. Albert Schweitzer, especially his religious beliefs expressed in "The Quest of the Historical Jesus."

I answered each of those letters and finally agreed to meet him at Chastain Park. At first, it was merely walking together and stolen kisses.

Soon, Grant asked me to meet him at a friend's house, but I told him that wouldn't do. His reaction was, "Well, I will rent us a place." And he did. He rented a gorgeous penthouse apartment in Buckhead, one with all the luxuries that life could afford.

The relationship evolved into a love affair, an affair between two married people. He was keenly aware of the loneliness in his life, and he awakened in me an awareness of my own loneliness and need for excitement.

Over time, I became aware of how wealthy he was and how extensive his business interests were. His avocation was raising horses, and he was an avid rider. Grant also liked flying and piloted his own plane. But money was not enough for him nor was having two children. He was an unhappy man, married to an alcoholic, instead of the adventurous mate he craved.

My life was quite different from Grant's. I was married to a good man, one totally immersed in his work and struggling to establish his architectural business. My needs were not important to John – at least not top priority. So, I was on the periphery of my husband's life, while I had become the focal point of Grant's.

What I was experiencing was something totally new to me: the intrigue of an affair, the devotion of a dashing man, as well as a skilled and ardent lover who would have bought me anything I even hinted that I might like. Grant showered me with gifts, but I never took any of them from the penthouse. Everything stayed there, except for one present, a horse. It was a white quarter horse and a handsome animal. I took riding lessons but was never good at it. In truth, I was always scared when I was on that animal.

For two years, we met when we could, which was the day when the housekeeper cared for the children. They came first. We might meet at the penthouse or take an afternoon flight to Callaway Gardens in his plane. It might be a trip out of town, one where I used my mother as cover and confidante.

With my European background, I probably approached the situation totally different from the way an American woman would have, at that time. In truth, physical contact and the subtleties of love making were not part of John's nature. He had some sort of built-in resistance to showing his physical feelings. To him, the sex act was something that should be consummated fast and in the dark, something you didn't talk about. Perhaps this was part of his Bible Belt rearing. Obviously, my passionate nature and his were not well matched. It was, therefore, easy for me to fall for a sexually attuned, handsome man, one who lived to please me.

The only people with whom I could share knowledge of what was happening in my life were my parents. I had been open with them, regarding my relationship with Grant, from near its beginning in 1959. Both understood and accepted our affair and kept my confidence. However, after I took Grant to their apartment in the Howell House to meet them, my mother later took me aside and said that she considered our romance a passing thing, nothing permanent. She admired John's stability and ambition and felt deep down that my relationship with Grant was wrong.

She discouraged me from marrying him and starting a new life in South America. Yet, on one occasion, she allowed Grant and me to accompany her to Miami, when she traveled there to visit friends. It gave Grant and me a chance to get away together for a few days for a tryst. Perhaps my mother felt that an extended time with Grant would help us get each other out of our systems. But, it didn't work that way. In 1961, two years into the relationship, I faced having to make a decision between two very different men and two very different lifestyles.

Grant was determined to get away from the unhappiness in his life. He wanted both of us to get a divorce, marry, and live our lives together in the open. Furthermore, he wanted us to go to Argentina or Brazil and start all over.

I was very tempted but told him I would have to think about that. He countered with, "I have to fly to Mexico on business. When I come back, I expect you to give me an answer."

I thought long and hard during the days after Grant left, finally deciding no, I was not leaving John. Here was a man who had been poor, who was trying to build something with no resources and no money. As difficult as our relationship was at times, I felt I could not walk out on him. My decision was made. And, it was final. I would tell Grant when he came back to Atlanta.

I never had the opportunity to give Grant my answer. On his return flight from Mexico, his plane crashed, and Grant did not survive. If he hadn't been an important man, I'm not certain how I might have learned any details about the accident. However, since he was prominent, I learned of his death while reading the morning newspaper.

I assume a business contact, someone in his confidence, took care of disposing of the penthouse, the jewelry, and other gifts that I left there, but no one ever contacted me. All I knew was what I read in the paper and that part of my life was over.

After Grant's death, I was extremely depressed and needed to get away, to clear my head, to refocus my thoughts and goals. After making arrangements for the care of my girls, I took some of my earnings from the French and Spanish classes I taught at the YMCA and headed for a summer of study in Spain. There I hoped to have time to gather my thoughts and consider how to best focus my interests and efforts.

You may wonder why I choose to tell about this episode in my life. It's because it was a major turning point, a moment in time when I found myself forced to evaluate the importance of the people in my life and vice versa. It was also a time to assess what Grant saw in me and how our relationship even began. He lived a life that placed him in the presence of scores of glamorous, sophisticated women who would have jumped at the opportunity to become his wife or mistress. Looking back on some of his comments, I believe the challenge he saw in me was my naivety and my genuineness. That was my greatest appeal, my *joie de vivre*.

While it is impossible to cling to naivety, I knew that being genuine was something that I could hold onto. This brought up the quandary of whether to continue keeping John in the dark about what had transpired for the previous two years. At the time, it might have made me feel better to tell him, but how would that make him feel? In order not to hurt him, I decided that silence was the best option. Confession would undo all that I had chosen to do.

1961

The U.S. breaks off diplomatic relations with Cuba, U.S.-trained Cuban exiles attempt an invasion of Cuba at the Bay of Pigs, U.S. Senate becomes concerned about John Birch Society activities, the Berlin Wall is constructed, and Ben-Gurion forms a new coalition government in Israel. The lives of Ernest Hemingway, Gary Cooper and Anna Mary Moses ("Grandma Moses") come to a close. John Steinbeck's *The Winter of Our Discontent*, Irving Stone's *The Agony and the Ecstasy*, and James Baldwin's *Nobody Knows My Name* are published, and the favorite songs are "Moon River," "Where the Boys Are," and "Love Makes the World Go 'Round." Freedom Riders test and force integration in the Southern States, Moscow synagogues are closed, the Trans-Siberian Railroad is electrified, and the Orient Express makes its last journey from Paris to Bucharest for many decades.

I Try Bullfighting in Spain

For some time, I had known about a summer class program offered at the University of Madrid. There I could study Spanish literature. John knew I was deeply depressed, but not the cause. He encouraged me to take the summer off, and the opportunity was more than tempting. My mother was more than willing to look after my girls and encouraged me to continue my education. I headed for Madrid.

There I was, an Atlanta housewife, running away from a bull in Madrid – when all I had planned to run away from was my husband and two children, when I left them at the Atlanta Airport two weeks before.

I was taking a four-week course at the University of Madrid, a long-cherished dream finally come true, and that particular day found me amid a group of tourists visiting a bull-breeding ranch on the outskirts of the city. It is there that *novilleros* or novice bullfighters practice to become full-fledged matadors, with the exception that, at the farm, the young bull is not killed, only teased.

Of course, when the owner of the farm asked for volunteers, I said to myself, why not? I may never have another chance to do that. Before I knew it, I was in the middle of the arena with a cape in my hand, flanked by the two *novilleros*. The young bull didn't look so innocent at close range. He was coming straight in my direction. This was no time for flirting! I dropped the cape and did what any sensible person would do: ran for dear life, only to fall into a nice pile of compost. But, who cared? Everyone was cheering the brave señorita!

From this experience, I learned to leave bulls alone, and while in Spain I also learned many other things, as well.

True, I had a great advantage over the ordinary tourist. I could speak Spanish, having lived in Cuba for several years. But, Cuba was a far cry from Spain!

Soon I discovered that the key that opens many doors when traveling is not the dollar! The language – even a slight knowledge of the foreign tongue along with good manners – is the best way to promote good will.

For example, when I first landed in Spain along with the other 120 passengers, including Hedda Hopper, everyone was clamoring for attention while we had to stay in line to pass through customs. I was so exhausted, I left the line and approached a policeman, asked him in my best Spanish to please check my bags and put me on a bus to Madrid. *"Por favor, señor"* turned out to be magic words; for when he heard them, he beamed all over. He didn't even open the bags but stamped my passport and showed me the way to the bus.

I was amazed to see how in Spain even in small restaurants and hotels most of the help could speak three languages. On the other hand, most American tourists, with few exceptions, don't even take the trouble to learn some basic sentences, such as "*Muchas gracias,*" "*por favor*" and "*No hay de que.*"

It embarrassed me to hear Spaniards remark about the bad manners of some American tourists. I didn't even want to be associated with the average American who usually looks carefully at his plate, puts his glass to the light, scrutinizes his fork and brags about how much better the food is back home. He insists on ordering American coffee and even asks if the water is pure at deluxe restaurants.

The adjustments I had to make were astonishing. The first two nights at the residencia were hectic. The University of Madrid is coed, and so was my dormitory – *and* its restrooms. The bathroom door didn't lock. Imagine trying to take a shower with people walking in as if it were Grand Central Station!

The guitar strumming of "La Paloma" at three o'clock in the morning and Beethoven's 9th Symphony around four gave me a little more musical appreciation than I could take.

After 48 hours of bedlam, I left in despair and moved to a nearby hotel in order to get some sleep – and a private shower.

While in Madrid, I acquired a new set of eating habits. I didn't begin dinner until ten p.m., which was considered "early" by Spanish standards. Movie theaters usually have two features: one at seven p.m. before dinner and one at eleven p.m. after an "early" dinner. But, most nightlife never begins before midnight. At the University, lunch was served around two-thirty and was never completed before four in the afternoon. And, siesta time is a souvenir I wish I could have imported to Atlanta.

The food in restaurants I found very good with as many as eight courses, varying from 60 to 180 pesetas ($1 to $3). It took almost an act of Congress for me to bring the waiter to the table with the next course or even the bill, and to get a glass of water, I seriously thought I would have to go down on my knees. Of course, their philosophy is who wants water when wine can be had for only 15 cents a bottle?

Speaking of wine, it was odd for me to see students and teachers refresh themselves with every kind of beverage, ranging from soft drinks to scotch, which was sold at the ever-present bars in dormitories and classroom buildings. Yet, I never saw a drunken Spaniard. The only drunks I saw while in Spain were – you guessed it – Americans.

It's just as well my husband didn't happen to walk in one evening when Julie, an American girl from New York who also studied at the University and I were having dinner at one of the most exclusive restaurants in Madrid. We were watching elegantly clad couples dance, when suddenly – and I don't know from where – there appeared at our table two guys who looked like twins. They were identically dressed in black shirts, red ties and checked coats. They looked more like two little Napoleons representing the local Mafia as they bowed low and asked us to dance: *"¿Baila usted?"* Thinking it was a custom, we accepted the invitation. They immediately became so amorous that we left them in the middle of the dance floor contemplating each other.

I learned that the average Spaniard, although poor, manages always to have enough money and enough time for a good meal. His dinner and his aperitif at the outdoor café provide an inexpensive pleasure and an important part of his life. His insouciance is quite relaxing. Perhaps it explains the lack of psychiatrists in the telephone directory. His disregard of punctuality is another of his characteristics. The only function that begins on time in Spain is the bullfight.

The pastime I enjoyed most was sipping a sangria while sitting at the sidewalk café and watching the people go by. Sangria, a popular drink, is made of iced red wine mixed with soda, lemon and sugar and served in a jug with a wooden spoon to stir it.

I was struck by the fact that the Spanish are all much smaller than Americans. I liked to see the couples walking by with their arms around each other. Actually, the men leaned on the girls with a proprietary air. Most Spanish girls wear no makeup at all or too much – and they like to wear pleated skirts with over blouses that tend to look like maternity frocks because their waists are rather large. Most men wear a traditional royal blue *guayab-erra* sport shirt. But what usually brought a smile to my lips was the way people carried a purchase, especially when it happened to be a fish. I could see the fish's tail sticking out from a newspaper underneath a man's arm.

I used to wear low heels and carry my high heels in a flight bag. Then, before entering a fancy place, I'd stop and change shoes. It's the only way to walk comfortably in Old Madrid, which is a confusion of narrow cobbled streets. Just to walk into the hundreds of different stores was an endless delight to me. I learned not to walk in, buy, pay, and leave. I discussed, bargained, argued, and exchanged ideas just as they did, as shopping be-came a challenging expedition in human intercourse.

Most Spaniards associate Atlanta with *Gone with the Wind*. They were amazed when I told them that the lunch hour here is literally one hour – or less. Our high standard of living never ceased to interest them, but segregation was something they did not understand, since there is no race problem there.

By the way, Hemingway's death was discussed everywhere. A bull breeding ranch owner told me he had met Hemingway and agreed with him about his criticism of Manolete, the great bullfighter. In Hemingway's last book, *The Dangerous Summer*, Manolete became a matter of great controversy in Spain. There the slightest criticism of bullfighting by an outsider is rarely permitted; therefore, Hemingway's last book will not appear in Madrid's bookstalls. Also, I overheard that Hemingway had reservations at Pamplona for the festival but cancelled two days before his death.

The *bedel* was the most colorful individual I saw at the University. He was the man who came in five minutes before class was over and like a zombie intoned two words: *la hora* (the hour), which meant that the class was over. This fellow took his job so seriously you'd think he was announcing a world-shaking event.

Very few places are air conditioned in Madrid, and all women carry their own "air conditioner," the traditional fan. I bought a fancy black lace fan and proudly fanned myself all through the literature class, only to have the professor tell me with a grin that my fan was an "evening fan." I learned that there is a fan for every occasion.

I felt safe when walking in the streets after 11 P.M. because the *sereno*, a civilian policeman, patrols the streets of Madrid. He would even open my front door, in the event I had lost my key.

Riding in a bus once, I casually asked the man sitting next to me, "What is that beautiful building?" He started to tell me the history. When I tried to interrupt his running commentary in order to tell him I had to get off, he got off with me so he could continue explaining about that building. I was 30 minutes late for a lunch engagement, but I know everything about the Palacio Real. Just ask me something.

I shall never forget the ride I took in an electric train from Seville to Granada. It took six hours to go about 160 miles. It was so shaky the roller coaster is nothing compared to that train – everybody got train sick; so, my pills for motion sickness, which I passed out, became the wonder drug.

The train stopped each time the conductor was hungry, thirsty or had a friend in the station. This one must have been very popular.

Equally memorable was the Festival of the Flamenco Music – something like a variety show. Only there you have public participation, just like at the bullfight. All yelled, "*¡Olé!*" applauded and threw cigarettes and cigars if they liked the performance. I even caught myself throwing American "filter" cigarettes, which I usually reserved for tips.

A month in Spain gave me a different outlook and an appreciation of the nobility and individuality of the Spaniard.

John's Farm

The same summer that I spent in Spain, John decided to fulfill one of his dreams and bought a 280-acre farm near Calhoun, Georgia. A road runs through the middle of the property, and it is most certainly a beautiful spot. One side is in forest, the other had been developed. For the cleared side, John designed a cabin to his liking and hired a contractor to build it for him. John loved it there and spent most of his weekends at the cabin. No phone, no interruptions, it was his way of totally removing himself from the pressures of work. He enjoyed the farm life and went into the cattle business, raising Black Angus. Since cattle require continual attention, he arranged with a neighbor to tend the herd while he was at work in Atlanta.

I didn't enjoy the farm much, but it was sheer joy to John. The few times my parents went there with us, I put them up in a nearby motel because of the cabin's small size and the field mice that kept insisting on moving in. John's dream was to build a house on the farm, but we haven't gotten around to fulfilling that dream. The cabin and forty acres were later sold to pay for our sailboat. We kept the rest of the farmland, and John continually expands and keeps tending to his orchards.

He uses a farming technique that must be unique to his family. None of our friends have ever seen anything like it. In the same breath, I'll tell you that it looks terrible ... and works. All of our newspapers are bundled and transported to the farm. There they are spread out to cover the ground and sprinkled liberally with water to keep them from blowing about. As they disintegrate, they smother the weeds, while allowing water to pass through to the ground. Furthermore, they help prevent ground moisture from evaporating. In short order, the paper becomes mulch, which helps the trees thrive. This is John's version of organic farming.

Part III

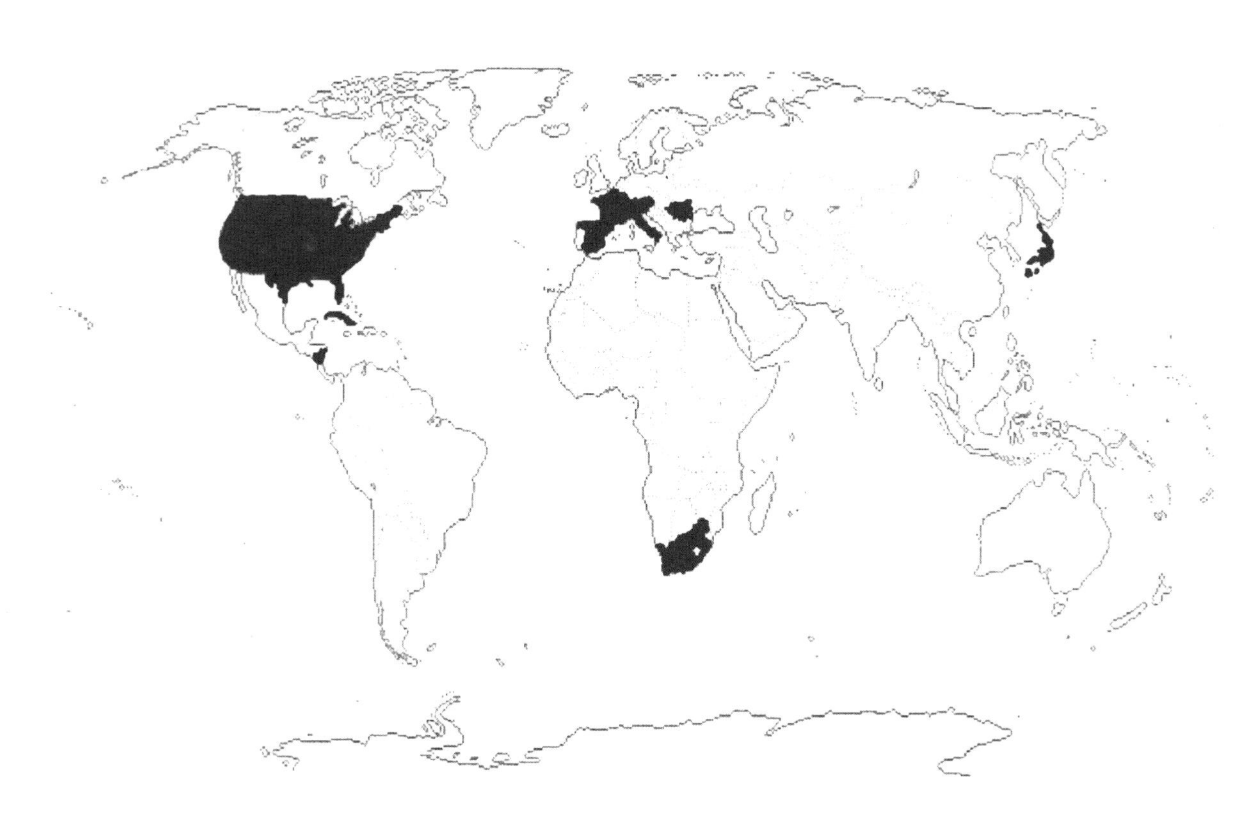

1963

The Civil Rights movement builds, and 200,000 black and white "Freedom Marchers" descend on Washington. U.S. and U.S.S.R. agree on "hot line" from the White House to the Kremlin, De Gaulle fights and succeeds in blocking Britain's entry into the Common Market, and United Arab Republic, Syria and Iraq agree to a union. President John F. Kennedy is assassinated by Lee Harvey Oswald, who is shot and killed by Jack Ruby, while America watches in horror as it happens on live television. Lyndon B. Johnson assumes presidency. John Le Carré's *The Spy Who Came in from the Cold* and Jessica Mitford's *The American Way of Death* become the books to read and discuss. Leonardo da Vinci's "Mona Lisa" travels to the U.S. for an exhibition, triggering an international exchange of art exhibits. The art and design world "rediscovers" Art Nouveau, and folk singers, especially Joan Baez and Bob Dylan, turn popular music towards protest and political messages. At the movies, we laugh at *Tom Jones* and are scared by *The Birds*. Hurricanes devastate E. Pakistan (22,000 killed) and Cuba (4,000 killed).

Becoming Consul

How I became an honorary consul for Costa Rica is a mix of happy accident and a willingness to grasp opportunities that came my way. In 1963, if you referred to Senator McKinley Conway, you might get a blank stare. However, if you said "Mac Conway," everyone knew that name. He was an Alabama native and Georgia Tech graduate who had distinguished himself during World War II. In the sixties, he became the power behind the World Development Federation.

John and I had been invited to a reception that Mac Conway was hosting for a delegation from Costa Rica, which was headed by that country's Minister of Industry, Hernan Garron. The reason for the visit was a proposed project in Costa Rica that was a result of President Kennedy's *Alliance for Progress*, a program for which I was doing some work.

When John and I were introduced to Hernan Garron, I greeted him in Spanish, which sparked a conversation that went beyond the basic party chitchat.; therefore, He and I learned we had a great deal in common. For example, this handsome, distinguished, silver-haired gentleman's grandfather had come to Costa Rica from France. When he learned of my French background, his black eyes sparkled and he shifted from Spanish to French.

At some point, Mexico came into our conversation, and I told Garron that, through a second party, Mexico had approached me about serving as their Honorary Consul. When he heard that, he quickly said, "Wait a minute, now. You haven't accepted, have you?" When I told him I had not, he said, "What about Costa Rica? We would love to have you represent us."

I wasn't certain what I should do or about the protocol involved or which I wanted to pursue – if either. When Garron learned that I had not formally accepted, he earnestly urged me to make Costa Rica my choice. He even went into detail about their current situation. While Mexico did not, at the time, have an honorary consul in Atlanta, Costa Rica did – if only in name. A highly connected Georgia Tech student held the title from Costa Rica who used his title primarily for special parking privileges. Costa Rica needed someone who could and would actively work for the country. "As soon as we return," he assured me, "I'll contact our Foreign Minister and recommend you, if you are interested."

I told him I'd have to think about it and discuss it with my husband, but deep down, I knew it was what I wanted. Both countries paid the same to their

Honorary Consuls: zero, zero, zero. At best, it would be a break-even proposition. One thing led to another, and I finally accepted Costa Rica's offer.

1964

The year of the Beatles: "I Want to Hold Your Hand" appears on the Billboard charts, *Meet the Beatles* is released, the press coins "Beatlemania" upon the arrival of the lads to America, Ed Sullivan brings them into living rooms across the country, and *A Hard Day's Night* introduces the band's unique blend of humor, wholesomeness, and phychydelia to audiences. While American teens are fawning over the adorable diplomats from across the Great Lake; France and the People's Republic of China agree to establish diplomatic relations. Later that year, China begins testing atomic bombs. Nuclear weapons production is cut back in the US and USSR by simultaneous declarations made by President Johnson and Premier Khrushchev, but this plan is counteracted on October 14th, when Leonid Brezhnev assumes power over the deposed Khrushchev. In Great Britain, thirteen years of Conservative rule ends with the election of the Labour Party. America's Defense Secretary, Robert McNamara, promises South Vietnam more military and economic aid against Communist aggressors, sparking protest, including the arrest of over 800 students at a Berkley sit-in. Nevertheless, the total number of US forces in Vietnam is over 1,000 and incumbent president Lyndon Johnson agrees upon a two-phase bombing plan. Stanley Kubrick alternately frightens and shocks moviegoers by making them laugh at the absurdities of war in *Dr. Strangelove*. Dr. Martin Luther King, Jr. also stresses the absurdity of war and racial injustice when he accepts the Nobel Peace Prize. Far away, the peaceful country of Costa Rica begins their struggle against the deadly thick ash spewing from the mouth of the centuries dormant volcano, Irazu.

Land of the Turtle and the Volcano

Once I accepted the Honorary Consulate appointment, I received an official invitation to Costa Rica, and John went with me. We flew Pan American. Unfortunately, when we reached San José, we couldn't land because of a big storm. I later learned that San José had a terribly positioned airport. The surrounding mountains created a dangerous downdraft, and during their rainy seasons, there are times, almost daily, when the fog prevented any landings.

Our plane turned toward Panama. After spending the night there, we returned to Costa Rica and better weather the next day. During the storm, there had been a welcome delegation of dignitaries at the airport, awaiting our arrival. But, the next day, when we finally could land, all we were greeted by was sunshine. No dignitaries were to be found.

I pulled out my list of phone numbers and called Hernan Garron, and the VIP treatment began. A car and chauffeur were sent to take us to our hotel, where we would be guests of the country.

Our first visit to Costa Rica was a fantastic experience. The little country of 3.5 million people rolled out the red carpet for this nobody. Because Hernan Garron was most definitely a *somebody* in his home country, we received royal treatment.

Hernan Garron's grandfather had sailed, at age 17, from France to California, then traveled on to Costa Rica by horseback. There he went into business making soap, something that had to be imported. Prior to his arrival, most people had no choice but to do without. His soap factory prospered and financed other family ventures, including becoming the local bottler of Coca-Cola in Limon.

The Garron family was highly respected and influential, the blue bloods of Costa Rica. Nearly all the men held or had held high political offices, and Hernan Garron even ran for president.

While we were guests of Garron's beautiful Costa Rica, I had a football game dedicated to me. (When I say *football*, I mean the game called *soccer* in the States). As guest of honor at the game, I was expected to kick the first ball, which I did in a hat and high heels. Tiny Rose must have looked ridiculous, surrounded by the tall players, especially since my kick sent my shoe flying , but the ball only a few feet across the field.

Rose being presented at the Costa Rican *Football game in her honor.*

Receptions, dinners, and entertainment filled our entire week. While in San Jose, I met President Orlich, who officially recognized me as Honorary Consul.

President Francisco J. Orlich's office is elegant, but in a demure way. While talking with the head of state in a very relaxed atmosphere, I suddenly felt this man's greatness. He had the gift to put one at ease.

When I handed him the polished piece of Georgia marble, a symbolic memento from Atlanta, he read the silver engraved inscription attentively: *"To Don Fancisco J. Orlich, President of Costa Rica with friendship, from the people of Atlanta, Georgia, U.S.A."*

Passing his hands slowly over the two embedded Kennedy coins, he looked up appreciatively. The coins had a special meaning for him. President Kennedy visited Costa Rica in March 1963, at the meeting of Central American presidents. Here, as in so many other countries, he was greatly loved, mourned, and missed.

I talked to many Costa Ricans from all economic levels. I had read that these people are our best friends, and now that I have met them, I am truly convinced.

Not once did I hear an anti-American feeling expressed. Costa Ricans all impressed me with their genuine admiration and loyalty for the U.S.A. They model their way of life after ours. It is obvious, viewing their lives, that democracy is more than just a slogan to them.

Costa Rica is considered politically, economically and socially stable to an extent not approached by any other country south of the border. Education surely must have accomplished that. Nowhere else in Latin America have I seen such ambition to learn and to work. Education is made available to everyone, even in the most remote parts of the country, with the result that illiteracy is only five percent. The government allocates almost 23 percent of its budget for education, believing there must be "more teachers than soldiers."

The Costa Rican army was abolished in 1948 during the social revolution. All forts and army camps now are museums and schools.

We wanted to see as much of the country as possible, and Hernan Garron, Minister of Industry and our host, made sure we did.

I equipped myself with scarves, sunglasses, umbrella and raincoat as protection against the dreaded blue-black volcanic dust Costa Ricans called "ceniza." A steady rain of fine ash poured from the angry mouth of the Irazu for nearly two years, covering San Jose, the capital city almost daily. The eruptions began again after centuries of slumber.

The ash collected on rooftops, in the streets, and clogged gutters, carburetors and fuel lines. It drifted into closed windows and doors and penetrated all machinery. It caused much of the coffee crop to die, and buried the nation's best milk producing area under three feet of compacted ash. Irazu damaged twenty square miles of the country.

Volcano dust irritates one's eyes and can cause eye and lung infections. I often wore sunglasses in the evening, and I bundled myself very thoroughly on the day we traveled to the crater's mouth.

We journeyed twenty-five miles from the capital on a good highway, our little four-wheel drive vehicle climbing unsteadily up a hazardous incline as we approached the big monster above. At 11,300 feet above sea level the air was quite chilly. The smoke and ash, which poured from the volcano's orifice, did not substantially add to our warmth.

When the road disappeared, we pushed through thick ash. It was like driving on a deserted beach cut with deep grooves by the heavy rainfall.

We heard deafening explosions, louder and noisier as we came closer, recurring every few minutes.

A thundering explosion occurred just as I reached the edge of the awesome abyss, which was almost two miles wide. I watched a huge black cloud of smoke and ash mixed with a deluge of incandescent rocks heave into the air. I felt the fear one must feel at witnessing an A-bomb explosion. I stood motionless and viewed nature's strength, feeling as insignificant and helpless as an ant that might be crushed.

The nearby land, once a lush pasture, now had been transformed into a vast wasteland of gray ash. The surrounding earth, with its mantel of death thrown over everything, was stripped of all but the silhouettes of lifeless trees bending under their load of ash.

The power that destroyed one of Costa Rica's most fertile areas was challenged by a greater power – that of the people's fine endurance and character. Armed with brooms, mops, rags, and hoses, people everywhere cleaned in defiance of the dust that continued to fall.

I traveled approximately 6,000 miles to meet this volcano. I am glad that I did, for since December 1964, the violent Irazu volcano, which damaged tiny Costa Rica almost daily, has slowed down and now has stopped completely.

The volcano represented but part of my adventure. We then motored 75 miles from the capital to the Pacific coast, passing through the major part of the central plateau. Here one finds the highest population density, where most of the coffee beans are cultivated. Driving through pineapple country, we could stop by the roadside and quench our thirst on a juicy fresh pineapple for just fifteen cents. In Puntarenas, the second largest port, we saw several merchant boats from Japan. The beach is black volcanic sand, but this doesn't discourage the swimmers.

Other regions in Costa Rica must be reached by air, using small landing strips that have been cut into the jungle. We arrived at Tortugero, a small beach on the Atlantic coast, in this way. Tortugero, the breeding spot of the huge green turtle, site of the University of Florida's experiment station, also contains a fairly primitive village that lies between the Atlantic Ocean and the lagoon.

An enterprising American couple who wished to retreat from civilization built a two-story army barracks-type hotel on the beach. The Green Turtle Inn, with its eight austerely furnished rooms and a single bath, is famous for its formidable cuisine. Room and the three best meals you could find anywhere cost but $10 per day, but your bed is likely to be an iron cot.

Tortugero gave us a jungle treat - a fresh coconut, split with a machete and mixed with rum. After dinner Hernan, John, and I walked on the beach. We watched the moon's reflection in the Atlantic Ocean, while Hernan told of his plans, hopes, and vision for his beloved little country.

"We have a primeval forest with a storehouse of products," he reflected. "This is a country for a technical pioneer. We need someone with courage and determination to beat back the jungle and make her give forth her wealth.

"This is the story all over my country, a story of underdeveloped mineral resources in the mountain area; underdeveloped cattle ranches in the rich Guanacaste region, underdeveloped tropical fruit industry, and – saddest of all – underdeveloped human beings. We are poor in a country that is potentially rich," he concluded.

The next day we boarded another small aircraft for a trip to Puerto Limon and civilization, 30 miles away. Limon, the largest port in Costa Rica, is famous for the lobsters found by the thousands on the rocks in December.

That afternoon, we headed back to the capital and Hernan had another surprise for us. We boarded the historical train *Tortuga*, or turtle, which really lives up to its name. It took three hours to go 25 miles.

"What feats could be accomplished with proper transportation," I thought as I realized at every stop that the train was the greatest event of the day. It is literally a lifeline to hundreds of people living in that tropical region.

It was odd to hear British accents. Costa Rica's population of 3.5 million is but two percent black, but here the population originated from Jamaica and was 98 percent black. Minor C. Keith, an enterprising Yankee, built the railroad between 1872 and 1911. Its construction cost 4,000 lives. Jamaicans were brought in because they were the only ones able to resist fever, heat, and mosquitoes.

The train rocked and rolled through abaca fields, whose harvest would become fiber for rope. Huffing and puffing, it clattered to a stop. Boys stood in the rain, using banana leaves for umbrellas and sold soft drinks and snacks.

We switched to a shaky little car for a final trip through the mountains. We passed an area of wooded hills where bananas and coffee climb together, the bananas shielding the coffee plants from the sun. Soon, we graduated from a wild trail to paved road only about 25 miles from our comfortable beds.

When our jet soared toward home a few days later, I felt as if I had left part of my heart in Costa Rica.

1965

Lyndon Johnson is inaugurated 36th U.S. President, Charles DeGaulle is re-elected, Winston Churchill dies, and Black Muslim leader, Malcolm X, is shot in New York. There are race riots in Los Angeles and attacks on civil rights demonstrators in Selma. Tornadoes strike the Midwest; cyclones devastate E. Pakistan, and earthquake rattles Chile. World production of diamonds totals 342,000 carats, in two decades U.S. wage scales double, the first flight to circle the earth and pass over both poles is added to the popular *Guinness Book of World Records.*

Op art, Ian Fleming's James Bond books, support for anti-pollution laws, Ralph Nader's *Unsafe at Any Speed,* and the music of The Beatles become popular obsessions. At the movies, *Dr. Zhivago* and *The Sound of Music* are the big draws, while Norman Mailer's *An American Dream* and Robin Moore's *Green Berets* sell out at bookstores.

Downtown and the Chamber of Commerce

During the 1950's and 60's, downtown Atlanta was an exciting place. People went there to shop and to dine. Atlanta had, at that time, only one major mall, Lenox Square, which was located in what had been a cornfield. Lenox, a grand mall for its day, was located just inside the northern city limits, and it took several years for it to offer the public more than a cafeteria for dining. Downtown was still the place to be.

Perhaps, the first significant sign of Atlanta's interest in becoming an international city was the way the population embraced each new foreign restaurant that opened downtown. There were several French restaurants, which employed skilled chefs. Emile's was my favorite. The number and variety grew and grew. The opening of the Midnight Sun in the Peachtree Center complex, a Scandinavian restaurant where you could dine on truly foreign fare such as reindeer, marked the zenith of the downtown area. After that, the best restaurants moved out from the center of town, and most relocated in the Buckhead area.

The first-run movie theaters and the legitimate theaters were also primarily located downtown, as were the other sources of entertainment. In the 50's, the Henry Grady Hotel's Paradise Room was the premiere spot to see famous performers. In the 60's, the Regency's Atlantis became the place to be and be seen. Virtually all major companies were run from the heart of the city, as were the banks. And, in those days, Atlanta was the banking center of the South. Not so today, that title has been ceded to Charlotte, N.C.

But, we are talking about the 50's and 60's, a time when the combination of the best entertainment, restaurants, stores, and places to work were all located in the vibrant downtown area.

The idea of working in the heart of the city and becoming one of the movers and shakers had massive appeal to me. But, how to become a part of all that? What stakes did I have to get into the game? My languages, of course. My first stop was the Atlanta Chamber of Commerce.

In 1965, in my role as Consul of Costa Rica, I went to the Atlanta Chamber of Commerce to see if there was interest in establishing a sister city relation with San José. When I arrived for my appointment with the Chamber's general manager, Opie Shelton, I was ushered into his office and greeted by a man I immediately knew could open doors, a very determined man who could make things happen. One look at Opie Shelton's flushed face and piercing blue eyes, and I also knew that he was a man who liked to drink.

When I began explaining why I was there, he candidly asked, "What is a 'sister city'? I've never heard the term."

I explained that it was when a city in one country and another city in a different country became frequently and officially involved in exchanges of cultural and business information through forums, exhibits, performances, and visits. In short, sister cities participate in a wide array of actions that promote mutual understanding, development and trade. Without hesitation, he said, "We might want to do that." However, the Chamber never did become involved with sister city relationships until a special committee was formed for that purpose over a decade later.

Nonetheless, my visit to the Chamber was by no means a waste of time for either Opie or me. Knowing that I spoke multiple languages, he handed me a letter. As forthright as he had been about not knowing what a sister city was, he said, "Rose, I've lost the envelope to this letter and don't know where it came from. Can you tell me because we'd like to answer it?"

The letter was in French and came from Basil, Switzerland. I read it to him and extracted the information he needed in order to reply, then left to wait and hear the Board's reaction to my sister city proposal.

That night I kept thinking about what I had experienced. I was surprised that, with all its money and resources, a chamber of commerce for a city the size of Atlanta, a city that was the air, rail, and expressway hub of the Southeast had no international department. So, I headed for my typewriter and began drafting a proposal, a proposal for the addition of an International Department.

My proposal outlined a modest start. It was for a one-person department that operated part-time: Monday, Wednesday, and Friday, from ten in the morning until three in the afternoon. That was a schedule that best suited my plans because I wanted to be home when my children returned from school. I also assumed it would easily fit within the Chamber's budget. In the proposal I explained the type of functions and results I felt a fledgling department could accomplish for the city.

Opie Shelton and the Chamber's Board of Directors liked what they read and accepted my proposal. So, I went to work. In every sense of the word, I was a one-person department. I had no secretary and even had to share office space because I was technically under the Department of Economic Development and initially reported to the Department's director. My salary was small, but money was not my motive. Being granted the opportunity of doing something of consequence was the major appeal of the job I had dreamed up for myself. By the time I left the Chamber ten years later, in 1975, the operation had become a full fledged International Department.

Opie Shelton,
Atlanta Chamber of Commerce
General Manager

When I first arrived at The Chamber, it was then riding the crest of a wave of national notice, thanks to its award-winning *Atlanta Magazine*, and an image campaign that had greatly helped set Atlanta apart from the racial strife with which other Southern cities were saddled. The campaign hailed Atlanta as "*the city too busy to hate*. " In large part, the city lived up to that description. Atlanta experienced no riots. Public facilities, schools, theaters, and most restaurants were integrated without incident – and without the press's knowledge, when Mayors Hartsfield and Allen could manage it. The two major exceptions were *The Pickrick* owned by Lester Maddox and *Leb's*, a delicatessen. Both were rightfully subjected to pickets, sit-ins, and much press coverage as a result of their resistance to integration.

Occasionally, I worked with *Atlanta Magazine* and its one-of-a-kind editor, Jim Townsend. At official close of daily business, he and his staff usually migrated upstairs to the Commerce Club bar and continued working over rounds of drinks. It's a management style that's hard to fault, considering the extraordinary number of national awards they won and the positive attention they brought to Atlanta. They helped shape Atlanta and transform it into a major American city.

Two of those staff members, Anne Rivers Siddons and Bill Deihl, became best-selling authors. Another staff writer, Terry Kay, won the 2004 Townsend award; a literary fiction award founded twelve years ago in honor of Jim Townsend. The magazine's initial and awarding-winning art director, Bob Daniels, was lured away by *Esquire* magazine. Numerous contributors, such as Paul Hemphill, also moved on to national prominence as journalists, authors, and photographers. Townsend was a visionary who, despite his drinking habits, had the ability to draw other visionaries to his side and keep them on his staff, working for paltry sums.

As soon as I joined the Chamber's staff, I was taken to the mayor and the governor to learn their interests and priorities. Appointments they wanted with representatives of foreign governments were set, and I accompanied them to those appointments, often serving as translator for the local and foreign dignitaries. We were able to attract numerous foreign governments to Atlanta. During my decade with the Chamber, several major international relationships were formed. Not only did I play a role in their development; I certainly had a wonderful time doing it.

An important contribution I made was establishing a protocol office, designed to provide assistance to the emerging Consular Corps and foreign dignitaries who visited or did business in Georgia. To make certain that the customs of other nations weren't unintentionally violated, I contacted the Chief of Protocol in the U.S. State Department for advice and guidelines. They proved to be a great help.

As Director of the International Department, we welcomed the Career Consulate General Offices of Japan, Korea, Belgium, Canada and France. We paved the way for many more to come. I quickly became known as "Miss International." The title was a result of my languages, and I must tell you that the latter opened every important door in my life. They also opened many doors for Atlanta and its Chamber.

A favorite story that involved my language expertise was the visit of a delegation of businessmen from Romania. (The name of my homeland, *Rumania,* was changed to *Romania* when the Communist took control.) Any

Rose and visiting delegations from Sweden and Norway.
Photographs of award winning *Atlanta Magazine* covers behind.

foreign visitor who came to Atlanta as a guest of the State Department came through The Chamber. The visit of these Romanians, who were looking for business opportunities, was unusual at that time because visitors from Communist countries were rare. When the Romanians arrived at the Chamber and were ushered into my office, they started talking among themselves in their native tongue. One said to the other, "She's cute, isn't she?"

Not knowing exactly how I should handle the situation and dying to laugh, I excused myself and went to my boss's office. "Opie," I said, "I can't do this. Before I had an opportunity to let them know I speak Romanian, they started exchanging comments about my looks."

Opie pointed his finger at me and stared me in the eyes, "You get back in there and talk to them." I did, telling them that I spoke their language. They couldn't conceal their shock, and I hope they eventually found the situation as funny as I did.

Another encounter with Romanians was anything but comical. I received a call from a Dr. Morrison from Georgia Tech, saying that a high level meeting of scientists would soon take place in Atlanta, and he was in dire need of an interpreter. I said I would be happy to offer my services. Prior to the meeting, I also received a call from the F.B.I., informing me that, as I might expect, their government was closely watching the scientists, Dr. Bogdan, Dr. Iliescu, and Dr. Constantinescu. When I felt it safe to do so, the F.B.I. wanted me to tell the three that, if they wanted to defect, to call a certain telephone number they gave me.

When I went to the meeting, I took my mother with me to also help interpret and perhaps create a distraction while I passed along the phone number. Mama did her part, and I did mine. But, they never put the number to use because, as much as they would have liked being free of the oppression of Romania's Communist government, they would have to leave their families behind, which would place their relatives in great danger.

The meeting went very well, in spite of the fact that I was not accustomed to translating scientific terms and data. Mama and I enjoyed having the opportunity to simply chat with someone from "home," especially three highly educated and interesting people. We did our best to make them feel welcome during their first visit to the U.S. We tempered the tour of the usual sites dignitaries visit with a trip to The Varsity, the world's largest drive-in. However, we took them inside for the experience of ordering in the establishment's fast-food lingo. They tasted their first hot dog and hamburger, and were fascinated by the whole experience.

I had long since merited a private office, secretary and had made a name for myself in Atlanta and scores of foreign cities and governments.

The Chamber's offices were and still remain in the heart of downtown Atlanta. Then, perhaps more so than today, it was a highly prestigious operation, one capable of shaping the future. As in the 60's and 70's, its building still combines offices and meeting rooms on the lower floors with The Commerce Club's elegant banquet facilities and bar above. In that bar and in those dining rooms, multitudes of history-changing decisions have been made.

Prior to and during my decade at The Chamber, the city's business leaders formed something akin to a kitchen cabinet for the mayor. Their sound advice was delivered during informal meetings, then run by the City Council for approval and placed into action. Mayors Hartsfield and Allen successfully operated in this manner, building a foundation for growth and progress.

Rose in her office with Esther, her assistant

If I had a favorite among these movers and shakers who shaped Atlanta, it had to be Mills B. Lane, the head of what were then Citizens and Southern Banks. He was a short man with a tall, very tall image. Mr. Lane told me once, "If you want credit for what you are doing or did, go to the bank. That's the only credit that counts."

Mr. Lane's office was across the street from The Chamber. When you saw him in an elevator or crossing the street, he always wore sneakers and specially made ties that said *It's A Great Life*. Lane was an early riser who held staff meetings at 6 AM, and you had better be there.

I've never known of a more accessible bank CEO. His door was always open to absolutely anyone who wished to speak to him, no appointment required; however, you were expected to wait your turn – and you better have something to say. He was a hands-on type of person. One day, when I called his office, he answered the phone, which surprised me. I stammered, "May I speak to your secretary?" and he said, "My secretary's busy."

My favorite story involving him had to do with a fellow consul, Robert Bunzl, who represented his home country, Austria. Shortly after his arrival in the U.S. from England, where he had relocated when the Nazis moved into Austria, he walked into C&S Bank to open an account. The little man looked pitiful. His shirt was frayed around the collar, his suit was ancient, and his shoes looked like a hobo's. When he told the bank clerk that he wanted to open a checking account, the clerk looked him over and said, "Well, sir, you must have at least a hundred dollars to open an account."

Mr. Bunzl pulled a check from his tattered pocket and said, "Will 25 million dollars do?"

This was at least fifty years ago. You could almost add a zero to see that check's worth today. The clerk almost fainted and ran into Mills B. Lane's office to make certain Mr. Bunzl and his crepe paper fortune were properly welcomed to the bank.

1969

Richard Nixon is inaugurated 37th U.S. President and tours Western Europe. The first U.S. troops withdraw from Vietnam, U.S. citizens continue demonstrating against military involvement in Vietnam, Protestants and Roman Catholics wage street warfare in Northern Ireland, James Earl Ray sentenced for the assassination of Martin Luther King, Jr., DeGaulle resigns as President of France and Georges Pompidou is elected. Agatha Christie's *The Mousetrap* celebrates its 7,000th performance in London, art world stunned by Old Master prices being pushed into the multi-millions by Japanese collectors, and Pope Paul VI names 33 new cardinals while eliminating over 200 saints (including St. Nick) from the liturgical calendar. "A Boy Named Sue" and the songs from the musical *Hair* become listener favorites. Wilt "The Stilt" Chamberlain moves NBA stars up to super star status and salaries to match.

Travels With My Daughters

Vienna

In 1969, my Chamber duties opened the door for me to introduce our daughters to the experiences of travel. While I hadn't been successful in making San José Atlanta's sister city, I did play a role in developing a sister city relationship between Vienna and Atlanta. Because of my being head of the International Department of Atlanta's Chamber of Commerce, I was asked to travel to Vienna to deliver a gift from Atlanta's mayor to Vienna's mayor. John was all for my taking both girls with me for their first visit to Europe.

At the time, Sabena Airlines was launching its first international flight out of Atlanta; so, the girls and I flew Sabena to Brussels. After going through customs, our first stop was the home of a cousin of Mama's. The children had little opportunity to appreciate Brussels because it was cold and rainy during our entire stay, and the weather made sightseeing a chore, rather than a pleasure.

Both the weather and our experiences improved as our visit progressed. From Brussels, we flew to Lausanne, Switzerland. The city is such a beautiful experience. It's so clean, so well organized, and so thoroughly international.

We had an even better time in Bern. The president of the college in Bern, Dr. Victor Von Bery, and I had first met in Atlanta while he was involved in a grant-funded program at Georgia Tech. After his tour of the college, the girls and I toured the town and visited Bern's incredible zoo. Then, we were on our way to Vienna.

In Vienna, we had a visit with Herman Von Karjon, an Austrian friend of mine who was working at the American Embassy. As in the case of Victor Von Bery, I had initially met Herman in Atlanta when he was on a diplomatic assignment. Herman had two boys who were my daughters' ages, which made outings with them especially memorable for the girls. Since both girls rode horses, the Spanish Riding academy was the highlight of our stay.

But, Vienna was not all sightseeing for us. I had work to do. I met with the mayor of the city, and we exchanged gifts. Our meeting was written up in the papers there and back home. From Atlanta, I delivered to him a copy of *Gone with the Wind* and a Frabel glass sculpture of a branch of dogwood and an along with an invitation to visit our city when the dogwood trees that blanket Atlanta are in bloom.

Events such as these were more than photo ops. They built friendships and ties between cities, and encouraged travel. They also laid the groundwork for expansion of trade and creation of import/export laws that eventually benefited everyone.

From Vienna, the girls and I headed for Salzburg. I was particularly glad to have the opportunity of taking them to Mozart's home. Giving them an appreciation of European culture was my goal for our trip, and I believe that goal was reached. In addition to the culture and beauty of Europe, the trip included some somber reminders of the dark side of that continent's history. We visited Hitler's bunker, and in Paris, we stayed at a hotel across the street from the one where George, my parents, and I stayed while Papa desperately tried to obtain visas for us. Our Paris stay was rounded out with visits to the city's great museums and, of course, the Eiffel Tower.

Just before we were to return to Atlanta, Marcelle came down with a serious ear infection. The doctors told us that she could not stand the pain she would experience on the fifteen-hour return flight. So, we sailed to New York on the last voyage of *The France* before it became the property of Norwegian Cruise Lines. There were very few passengers on board, which proved to be our good fortune. We were upgraded to first class and experienced all the luxury that famous ship offered: dinner at the captain's table, magnificent food and entertainment, special activities for children, a party every night, and so much more.

By the time we reached New York a week later, Marcelle's ears were fine; so we were able to fly from New York to Atlanta, instead of traveling by train. This trip was only the beginning of our daughters' travels. In fact, as I write this, Marcelle is in her eleventh year of living just outside of Paris.

Romania

When countries didn't offer to cover my travel expense, the Chamber was not quick to pick up the check. For example, in the summer of 1969, Richard Nixon announced that he was going to visit Romania. This certainly captured my attention, as I had not seen my relatives in Romania since my parents, my brother, and I fled the country in 1939.

I went to Opie and said, "I want to go to Romania to visit relatives. If I go, representing *Atlanta Magazine*, I can get into part of the activities that involve the President's visit and bring you back an interesting story. Can you accredit me to have press privileges?"

Opie said, "Great! But I don't want to pay for it. I'll let you have a camera, film, and credentials, but that's it."

I said, “That’s fine. I never asked you to cover my expenses.” I didn’t tell him what a lousy photographer I was. And he never found out because I wasn’t allowed to take pictures while there.

My traveling companion for the trip was my ten-year-old daughter Marcelle. When we arrived via Swiss Air at Romania’s new Otopeni Airport, it was very difficult getting through customs and immigration. When they saw on my passport that I was born in what is now Romania, they became very suspicious, and when they learned I spoke their language, it got even worse. The longer I was there, the more I realized that, after being under Communist rule for so many years, everyone in Romania had learned to trust no one. Remember that Ceusescu was still in power. It would not be until 1989, after he was killed and a revolution had taken place that the Romanians would begin their slow, slow, slow recovery from the terrible things he had done to his countrymen.

Finally, we were allowed through customs and immigration. My mother’s sisters and the husbands of the two who were married came to greet us. It was as exciting for them as it was for Marcelle and me. I had not seen any of these relatives since I was a little girl. Aunt Frida’s husband, Stelian, was still an accountant and Aunt Fany’s husband, Beno, had a nondescript job. Aunt Aurica was still single; however, she did marry later.

The first thing my relatives said was how much they would like for us to stay with them; but that was not allowed. We would have to go to a hotel. I already knew about this governmental restriction. I thanked them for their offer and explained to them that we were staying at the Intercontinental. While it was considered the most expensive hotel in Bucharest, it was nonetheless shabby and dirty. If you asked for something, they would say “If you don’t like it, you can go to the hotel across the street.” The concept of service and putting one’s best foot forward was a dead concept. That’s Communism for you.

When we arrived at the hotel, my family had to remain outside. Romanians were not allowed to enter. Marcelle and I quickly unpacked, changed, and rejoined our waiting relatives. Even though we could not stay with them, we could visit. My aunts said, “Let’s go to our house. We still live at the same place.”

But, they didn’t live “at the same place” I remembered. When I left, they lived in my grandfather’s extraordinary house. Now my aunts and uncles, all five of them, lived in a wretched little apartment. Prior to their deaths, my grandparents also lived there. A total of seven people jammed into a two-bedroom apartment. Nonetheless, their living conditions seemed luxurious in comparison with the living quarters issued to many others. Their apartment had a bath and kitchen that were separated only by a partition. The eating area, which was in the kitchen, contained a sofa that doubled as Aurica's bed. Not being members of the Communist Party, they had been stripped of their home and their former wealth.

We went everywhere on foot or by bus because my relatives did not have a car – at least not those who met me at the airport. The one relative who did was Paul Daniel, a cousin whose nickname was Puiu. His mother was my maternal grandmother's sister. Puiu had served in the Communist army and parlayed his military record into party membership and great wealth. He not only had a car, it was chauffeur driven. Yet, when he heard I was coming, he did his best to keep his distance because he was very nervous about being seen with me. Even those on the inside of a police state aren't safe.

It was up to me to host everything my relatives and I did because they had no money. Furthermore, I later learned that if I had given them money it would have gotten them into real trouble. I was continually changing American money into *leis*, their currency. There were places, however, where U.S. dollars were welcomed. When I took them out to eat and showed my American passport, another menu was always produced, and the food choices greatly improved. I then paid in American dollars and was treated like a VIP.

It was a similar situation in stores. I took them grocery shopping despite their warning that they couldn't buy anything. It was forbidden. We went anyway. I would shake my passport in front of the clerks' noses and we could buy anything we wanted. When I left, it was with a virtually empty suitcase because I left most of my clothes for my aunts.

While there, I also reconnected with Dr. Bogdan, the nuclear physicist I translated for at the Georgia Tech conference during his visit to Atlanta. My aunts were uneasy enough about my visiting with him, but another incident that I did not instigate brought their quick and vocal disapproval. While waiting for my family to meet me, a man on a motorcycle handed me a note and drove off. It said, "I need your help to get to the U.S.A. Please meet me at the café across from the hotel."

My aunts weren't certain if the man was a would-be defector or some-one setting a trap for me. They were certain, however, that he was trouble and could land my daughter, my relatives and myself in prison. I did the safe thing and did not go to the café.

I had arrived in Bucharest two days before the Nixons were to arrive. People were still busy painting, trimming shrubbery, cleaning the streets, and preparing to make a big show. The plan was that I would go to the American Embassy the next day to get my accreditation. That night, after our dinner at the restaurant with my relatives, my plans suddenly changed when my daugh-ter became very sick with food poisoning. Instead of going to the U.S. Embassy for my press credentials, I spent the time trying to get medical attention for Marcelle.

Eventually, I figured out that no Romanian doctor was allowed to help us. Our only means of medical help was to go to – you guessed it – the American Embassy. I put her in a cab and took her there. By then, it was evening again. Nonetheless, an American doctor saw us and gave Marcelle some medication. It did work. But, not before what became Marcelle's most vivid memory of the trip. She threw up on the floor of the American Embassy.

If only I could have gotten my press credentials while I was there, but that would have been too easy. Such transactions had to wait until morning. Unfortunately, the next day was when Nixon was to arrive. By the time I got the much improved Marcelle to my aunts' apartment and returned to the Intercontinental to change clothes, there was no time to go to the Embassy.

I needed to head straight for the airport. Outside the hotel, I found myself standing in the middle of a swarm of reporters, not knowing what I should do. In the midst of all this confusion, I heard a British reporter quip, "At least Americans come in a plane. Russians come in a tank."

I was so dejected, tears started welling up in my eyes. Everyone was getting ready to go to the airport... everyone but *me*. I wandered out onto the sidewalk and saw a limousine with an American press banner on it. I ran to it and asked the passenger, "Are you going to the airport?" When he said "yes," I asked if I could ride with him.

The man gave me a funny look then said, "Sure. Get in."

I'm not revealing the man's name because what he soon did was illegal, and I don't want to cause trouble for someone who did me such a great favor.

When I got in, we started talking and I told him why I didn't have my press card. His eyes widened. "You speak Romanian?" When I told him I spoke it fluently, he exclaimed, "God sent you! Our interpreter is sick, and we don't have anyone who knows the language. Will you interpret for us?" When I told him I wasn't accredited, he said, "That's not a problem."

From under the seat, he produced a Polaroid camera and took my picture. Then he attached it to a card that said "White House Press." Handing it to me, he said, "Here. You're accredited. I want you to tell us everything anyone says. We know what Nixon's going to say, but we don't know what the Romanians are going to say."

We went to the airport, and I, with great excitement and happiness, began earning my ride and credentials by finding them a location that was far better than the one they had been originally assigned. From then on, it was like a spy movie. The Romanian cameras were trained on us. I translated everything that was said in Romanian to English for them, including a brief greeting that Nixon had memorized. They were very pleased.

On our way back to the hotel, the man from the press said, “You were wonderful, and I’m going to pay you five hundred dollars.” I declined his fee, saying that the experience was pay enough. He continued, “Well, at least let me give you the services of my driver for the next two days.” He instructed the driver to take me wherever I wanted to go.

Upon arriving in my aunts’ neighborhood, I suddenly saw one of them running towards the car, waving for the driver to stop. I was sure Marcelle had taken a turn for the worse. I quickly got out of the car and asked, “Aunt Aurica, is something wrong with Marcelle?”

She shook her head no. With panic in her eyes, she whispered, “You must send the car away – *immediately*!”

I laughed and replied, “No, you don’t understand. The car and the driver are for us. The driver will take us to the mountains tomorrow.”

Her fear became filled with anger. “*You* don’t understand,” she said. “We saw you on television, with a badge that clearly said ‘White House Press.’ You forget that this is a Communist country, a police state.”

Once again, I tried telling her that there was nothing to be upset about. In fact, there was. Neither the man from the press, nor I, knew that our driver was a member of the *Securitate*, the secret police.

My aunt succeeded in changing my mind when she added, “You could be jailed. You must leave Romania immediately or you’ll be arrested. You entered this country as a tourist, but they now know that you’re here for other reasons. You could be *jailed*!”

My daughter and I returned to our hotel, collected our bags, hailed a taxi, and headed for the airport. We were on the next Swiss Air flight out of Communist Romania. We returned with a great story – but with no pictures.

Later, I learned that the secret police were only minutes behind us. They came to the hotel, looking for “the spy,” then went to my relatives’ apartment. My aunts and their husbands were questioned under duress about my alleged role at the White House. Only because they were senior citizens, they were not incarcerated. Fortunately, my plane had taken off before the police thought to check the airport for us.

But that wasn’t the end of this adventure.

A few months later, an individual in a shabby gray raincoat came to see me at my office. He swaggered in, flashed his CIA credentials and said, “We know exactly what happened in Romania and would like to offer you a job. Please come to Washington for an interview. Here is your ticket.”

I was consumed with curiosity and a bit surprised at John’s reaction. “Go,” he said. “It appears to be an opportunity to serve your country.”

I went and was first presented with a language test, which I passed with no problem. Next, they asked me to follow them to another room where two men sat at a table. With little ceremony, they handed me a pad and pencil. “We want you to write down the highlights of your life up to now, and when you finish, we would like to ask you some questions.”

I wrote and wrote and wrote until I was very tired. When I gave them my scribbling, I asked, “What do you want to know, and what do you want with me?”

“We want you to go to some trade shows in Romania and just listen to what people say.”

“You want me to spy? Is that it?”

They shook their heads, “Not exactly.”

After a pause, one of them continued: “Look, Mrs. Cunningham, we know you have family in Romania. What we must know is this: if we entrust you with some sensitive information and you are arrested, would you divulge that information in order to save the lives of your family members, or would you remain quiet?”

I was suddenly very angry. I snatched up my purse, shouted, “You can go to hell!” and stormed out.

Shortly after I returned to Atlanta to resume my position at the Chamber, I received a letter from the CIA saying, “We regret to inform you that you failed the security test."

Romanian National Costume

Miscellaneous Duties

During the sixties and early seventies, Chamber officials and I made numerous trips to New Orleans to visit their various foreign consulates. Our goal was to interest foreign governments in opening offices in Atlanta.

When they came to Atlanta, we entertained them splendidly. Not everyone with whom I officially dealt fell into either the category of political figure or business leader.

One day a rotund French lady in her sixties, named Madame Gilberte Crognier, came to see me with a manuscript under her pudgy arm. She was vivacious and Gallic in every respect. With excitement and pride in her voice she said, "I've written a sequel to *Gone with the Wind*, and I want to meet Margaret Mitchell's brother."

The reference was to Stephen Mitchell, the lawyer who had zealously protected all rights associated with the novel. When I heard what she wanted, I told her that, prior to Ms. Mitchell's death, she had expressly stated that she wanted no one writing a sequel to her story.

That information did not faze the lady. "I want to meet the brother, to touch him, because I just love the woman in the book."

Finally, I agreed to contact Mr. Mitchell on her behalf and see what could be arranged. When I called him, I told him that the lady didn't understand that what she had done was illegal and asked him if he would at least meet her. He graciously agreed, and I took her across the street from the Chamber to his office.

He did not budge from his position concerning sequels. (Many years later, when he realized that an authorized sequel would protect the book and its characters from becoming public domain, he did change his mind.) Madame Crognier had her audience with Stephen Mitchell but returned to France without permission to copyright or print her book.

Nonetheless, she did print a few copies for family and friends. I was sent one of the copies for having done what I could for her. I must say she was an excellent writer. Her sequel took the characters from Atlanta to New Orleans to Charleston.

Some time after that, the film version of *Gone with the Wind* was re-released with considerable fanfare, including the appearance of the stars that were still alive. These included Olivia DeHaviland, Butterfly McQueen, and Victor Jory.

I remembered Madame Crognier and suggested to Mayor Ivan Allen that he send her an invitation and include her among the guests of honor. He did, and she gladly accepted. As a result of the invitation and our initial visit, this delightful woman and I became close friends.

Over time, I learned that my new friend was a published poet, who was born in Paris in 1904. In 1928, she served as aid to General Leclerc, and in 1940 became personal secretary to General Charles de Gaulle. Her life included travel in Africa from Cape Town to Cairo with the French army, as well as assignments that took her from Lebanon to Algiers. Her involvement with the military continued into 1945.

Through my Chamber duties, I became friends with another writer, Dr. Raimondo Luraghy, a historian from Italy. He was a short, blue-eyed gentleman who clearly liked his pasta. In 1966, he was commissioned by the President of Italy to write a book about the United States' Civil War. Dr. Luraghy needed contacts in Georgia, and he came to me for help. I arranged a dinner party for him to meet Atlanta's two leading authorities on the Civil War - Wilbur Kurtz and Franklin Garrett. Luraghy later described the evening as "going from the bottle to the battle."

There was much debate because Luraghy disagreed with Kurtz and Garrett concerning the locations of various battles, who perished where, and scores of other details. I have no idea who was correct about the various details or how Luraghy might possibly arrive here knowing more than two historians who had lived their lives walking the sites and studying all the original records. I did learn something few Southerners know - Lincoln had approached the famous Italian general Garibaldi and offered him command of the Union Army.

A year after the Civil War was "re-fought" around my dinner table, Dr. Luraghy published a 1,275-page book on the Civil War, complete with maps and a meticulous bibliography. He sent me a copy… in Italian.

Another favorite story involves my lack of knowledge, concerning the "great American pastime." During Ivan Allen's administration, he realized his dream of making Atlanta a major league sports city with the opening of the Atlanta Fulton County Stadium. It was a multi-use facility that could accommodate baseball, football, and soccer. In April of 1965, the opening exhibition baseball game stirred a great deal of attention nationally and internationally. It marked Atlanta as a major American city, and the international press showed up to see Mayor Ivan Allen, Jr. throw the first ball.

I was asked by Opie Shelton to accompany a portly French journalist, Monsieur DuPrée from "*Le Monde*," to the event and explain the game to him. It was like the blind leading the blind. To me the game meant someone takes a wooden stick, hits a ball, and then runs like hell while the multitude screams.

When the game started, he asked, "What are they doing?"

I turned around and asked the people behind me, "What are they doing? What are they doing?" They explained the action on the field to me, and then I translated the helpful fans' response into French for the reporter. The whole evening went that way. He asked question after question. Each time, I dutifully sought an explanation from the people behind us. They fed me information, and I translated their answers into French for the bewildered reporter.

He couldn't understand why people kept getting up during the game to go get hot dogs, Cokes, and beer. When one of the players broke his bat, the Frenchman cried, "I think you have to belong to some secret organization to understand this game. It's crazy!"

While at the Chamber, I was simultaneously continuing my duties as Honorary Consul to Costa Rica. My non-paying job came with honor, a diplomatic car tag, and free parking at the airport. My phone bills, travel expenses, stamps, stationery, and other incidentals were to a small degree offset by my being qualified to authenticate signatures and documents. I absorbed the sizeable balance. In fact, I even had to purchase my own stamps for documentation of birth certificates, marriage licenses, deeds, and similar legal papers. The service was similar to that of a notary public and carried a fee. Any documents passing my desk had to be stamped. I even had to pay my sizeable phone bill, travel expenses, and incidentals. John wasn't happy about the expense and encouraged me to resign several times. He also didn't enjoy the numerous receptions; however, I certainly did. And I worked hard for Costa Rica.

In 1975, the Organization of American States met in Atlanta. Gonzalo Facio, the Foreign Minister of Costa Rica, named me a member of the Costa Rican delegation. Facio gave Costa Rica's opening statement at the event - a speech that was typed in my living room on my typewriter. It was an exciting time. I got to know all the members of the delegation well, including the bodyguard who was posted at my door every moment that the Foreign Minister was inside. I deeply enjoyed working with the Costa Rican officials. They appreciated my efforts on behalf of their country – well, almost all.

In 1987, Dr. John P. Crecine, President of Georgia Institute of Technology, contacted me regarding a proposed project that would involve Georgia Tech and Costa Rica. The plan included formal establishment of a Georgia Tech coordinating committee to work with Costa Rica on activities of mutual interest. Among these was the creation of a satellite program for post graduate work in Costa Rica; the establishment of the Latin American Institute of Technology and the Foundation for Technological Research.

Oscar Arias
President of Costa Rica

My efforts on Georgia Tech's behalf culminated in a visit to Costa Rica in order for Dr. Crecine and his delegation to meet with President Oscar Arias, the Nobel Peace Prize winner of 1988.

RJR Nabisco offered the services of its corporate jet because the company's Vice Chairman, Robert Carbonel, was also the President of EARTH, an organization funded by RJR. EARTH was very much in favor of the programs that Tech was proposing. Fair skies and the deluxe plane got us to the VIP hangar at San Jose's airport three-and-a-half hours after takeoff.

The meetings went superbly, and I enjoyed translating for those who did not speak both languages. However, all their wonderful plans became the victim of timing. President Arias was in his last year of office, and a Costa Rican president cannot succeed himself. His successor was not interested in pursuing Arias' projects. The plans were canceled. Georgia Tech elected to set up a similar program in France. Petty politics cost Costa Rica what could have been a most valuable school and could have fostered stronger political and economic ties with the U.S.

On another trip, I organized the visit of officials from Marietta, Georgia, to their sister city of Heredia in Costa Rica. The leader of the group of Marietta citizens was Dr. Betty Siegel, President of Kennesaw State College, which is now Kennesaw State University.

On that trip we were greeted and hosted by the Vice President of Costa Rica, a gracious lady, Doña Victoria Garron de Doryan. She was also an educator, published writer and poet. Doña Victoria remains one of my dearest friends to this date.

In 1987, as Vice President of Costa Rica during Dr. Oscar Arias' administration, she visited Kennesaw State College to give a major speech on education and economics. As part of my duties as the Honorary Consul of Costa Rica, I arranged the entire visit. This included official visits with Georgia's then Governor Joe Frank Harris, Atlanta Mayor Andrew Young and a tour of the Georgia Institute of Technology campus. These momentous international exchanges paved the way for the present global initiative at Kennesaw State University, under the leadership of President Siegel.

Another political change that I deeply regretted involved me directly. The opposition party decided to open a career office here in Atlanta. That meant that I could not continue in my capacity as Honorary Consul because our State Department does not allow an honorary consul to work in conjunction with a career consul. So, in 1989, I had to resign. The new party in power sent three people to open an office. Together, the three did less than I had operating out of my home.

I still continue helping Costa Rica when the opportunity arises, as it did during the 1996 Olympics. Those details are covered elsewhere, but, I had the opportunity of helping their under-funded teams.

When one of the volcanoes in Costa Rica erupted, I got together over $50,000 worth of hospital equipment. The donations were from numerous hospitals in the Atlanta area. With the help of Carolyn Wills, a friend who was the public relations executive for Eastern Airlines in Atlanta, arrangements were made for complimentary air transportation of the equipment and supplies. Carolyn also contacted Channel 5 WAGA-TV in Atlanta and told them what I was in the process of accomplishing. The director of their special programming thought what I was doing would make an interesting special and offered to send news anchor Virginia Gunn and a television crew along to cover the event from collection through delivery.

The most difficult part of the operation was contacting the Costa Rican government to let the proper authorities know the time of the flight's arrival. After many calls and circumventing a number of bureaucratic hurdles, I was able to reach the First Lady of Costa Rica, Doris Monje. She took care of everything on her end, and Carolyn and I on ours; consequently, thousands of wounded Costa Ricans were helped.

When Carolyn, the Channel 5 news crew, and I arrived, I learned that Doris Monje was not on speaking terms with her husband, President Luis Alberto Monje. They communicated with one another only through a third party. We quickly rearranged the filming schedule in order to interview her in the morning and her husband in the afternoon.

Our interview with him was a brief one because he cut it short saying, "Let the three of us go to the Presidential Palace for a special session with Members of the British Parliament." With that, he took Carolyn and me by the arm and escorted us to his waiting car. President Monje, who had a Santa Claus physique, sat in the middle of the rear seat with Carolyn on one side and me on the other. I remember his chuckling and saying, "I always wanted to sit between a blonde and a brunette."

Carolyn, however, wasn't in a jovial mood. She was terrified, assuming that Costa Rica, like some of the Central American countries, considered political coups the national pastime and Presidential limousines made for target practice. You can imagine her relief when I told her that Costa Rica had no army and was the most peaceful country in this hemisphere.

Channel 5's crew returned with an interesting television special, Eastern Airlines created good will here and abroad, and it became clear to a great many important people that I could make things happen.

1971

A year of natural disasters: Tuscany, Italy is ravaged by earthquakes; the San Fernando Valley of California receives a quake that measures 6.4on the Richter Scale; a landslide in Peru kills over 200; Mt. Etna erupts on April 15th; India's Bay of Bengal is hit by a tornado and a tidal wave, killing 10,000. The violence of nature is echoed in films like *A Clockwork Orange* and *Dirty Harry*. But by and large, most people are striving for more peaceable times: the US, UK, and USSR outlaw nuclear weapons with the Seabed Treaty; a confederation is formed in the middle east between Syria, Libya, and Egypt; and the United Arab Emirates is formed in the Persian Gulf. When John Lennon recorded "Imagine" in 1971, could he himself imagine the gathering of half a million peace-loving protestors in Washington, DC on April 24th? In the South, the busing of students is ordered by the Supreme Court to help achieve racial de-segregation, and Atlanta, GA takes steps to become an international city with the completion of the Hartsfield International Airport.

Tokyo

At the Chamber, we prepared for the visits of scores of America's leading figures, such as Henry Kissinger, Robert Kennedy and for even greater numbers of ambassadors, heads of state, and royalty, including the crowned Prince of Denmark. Of them all, I would say that I found the Japanese delegations the most interesting. They clearly saw the mutual business opportunities.

Their coming to Atlanta might have been delayed many years if it hadn't been for John's and my visit to Japan, in 1971, as tourists. As usual, our travels were part pleasure and part business for me. It was the first time either of us had been to any part of the Orient. Even though we were not on official business, while there, we were guests of the Japanese government. I made an effort to add a little Japanese to my collection of spoken languages, which pleased the dignitaries we met.

From the moment even the most unobservant person steps off a plane in Tokyo, he or she cannot help but recognize how extremely different these people's approach to living is from ours. Their orderliness is amazing. Not a square inch of space is wasted. For example, as you travel their streets you glimpse tiny, manicured gardens that are tucked between buildings.

Japan is approximately the size of California, a state with a population of less than 20 million. Japan, on the other hand, manages to fit more than 90 million people in the same amount of space. With the exception of rush hour when people are packed into their highly efficient trains, there is little feeling of being crowded, even with 11 million people living in Tokyo.

Any and everything associated with business is efficient, but rarely hectic. Tranquility, orderliness, and grace are woven into everything the Japanese do. We quickly learned that foreign visitors receive priority over any domestic business. Even when we stopped by the office of Mr. Sigeo Nagano, the president of both the Japanese and Tokyo Chambers of Commerce, he left an important business meeting to join us for an elegant and leisurely tea, which was served in a special room for VIPs.

Cleanliness is close to being an obsession in Japan. Taxi drivers wear immaculate white gloves. Hotel maids scurry about wearing gauze masks. Businessmen and shoppers walk the main streets, wearing masks. Our Japanese host told us that the masked people we saw on the streets likely had colds and did not wish to risk spreading them. That may explain some of the masks, but I'm convinced that the majority wore masks because of the air pollution. Industrialization has blanketed the country in smog. We saw for ourselves that all the industrial cities shared the same problem. Even on what should be clear days, the crown of Mount Fuji is often hidden from sight by a cloud of pollutants.

At the time of our visit, Atlanta businessmen were eager to establish consular representation of Japan in Atlanta. The head of the Japanese Chamber agreed. "We need more visitor exchanges to learn about each other," he said. "We also need to find a profitable way of trading and experiencing industrial growth, while maintaining our traditions and our respect for humanity and beauty."

Atlanta felt the same way, and I was there to help prove the point. New Orleans had long been the traditional site for consulates in the Southeast. Situations were changing, however, and air transport was steadily cutting into the shipping industry's business. The increasing importance of air travel and Atlanta's unique position as the air hub of the South were making all countries without honorary or career consuls in Atlanta, rethink their strategy. Our city was the unquestionable air, freeway, and rail hub of the South.

The year before, Belgium moved its consulate general from New Orleans to Atlanta; joining the U.K., Israel, and West Germany. Costa Rica was among the seventeen countries with honorary consuls. Denmark, Israel and Canada's Ontario province also operated commercial offices. The Atlanta Chamber of Commerce's World Trade Council was eager to see every country connected with Georgia's capital city. Japan would be a strategic addition, one that would motivate others to follow suit.

While in Tokyo, Mr. and Mrs. Susa, friends of a Japanese girl who had visited us the previous Christmas, invited us to a luncheon at their apartment. We arrived there by train. John and I developed a great appreciation for the city's subway system - fast, clean, and efficient.

The visit to the Susa home was an excellent opportunity to learn more about how people lived. When we arrived and removed out shoes to enter, I was surprised to find their living room was Western in style. Their bedroom was not. It had the traditional Japanese straw mats, called *tatamis*, on the floor. I was told that the Japanese feel there is spiritual satisfaction from sleeping on the floor. I also learned that, since the floor was used for sleeping and sitting, dogs and cats were not considered appropriate pets. Instead, the Japanese prefer caged birds and exotic fish.

Other than the living room and bedroom, the Susa's apartment contained two other rooms, a bath and a kitchen. The bathroom was a new experience for us. The commode was at floor level. In her small kitchen, Mrs. Susa prepared us a special Japanese meal called a *Sunomono*. Radishes, carrots, cucumbers, mushrooms, raw shrimp, cold scrambled eggs, small bits of salmon, Japanese pepper sprouts, minced ginger, and mashed eggplant composed the dish's ingredients.

On other occasions, we were greeted with foods that take some getting used to for Westerners: raw jellyfish, raw shrimp, eel, and other delicacies that I could not and didn't particularly want to identify. Every dish prepared for us was presented with great attention to detail. We even had some of their famous Kobe beef. When traveling the countryside by train, I noticed that we never saw any livestock. On asking why not, we learned that their cattle are raised indoors, where they are fed beer and given daily rubdowns to produce the finest quality meat.

Their streamlined bullet trains, which travel at 125 miles per hour, provide a grand way to travel in air-conditioned comfort. We went by train to visit Kyoto's many temples and to tour Nagoya, the home of Toyota and Noritake. At the time we were there, the Noritake factory employed more than 6,000 people to make their china. We were told that the average worker earned $200 a month for 48-hour workweeks.

Part of my official business in Japan was to present a slide presentation to the officials of the Foreign Ministry and Finance Ministry. Its narration was in Japanese, and the presentation stressed the importance of Japan opening a Consulate General's office in Atlanta. We found officials of the Japan External Trade Organization (JETRO) were very familiar with the activities of Japanese businessmen in Atlanta.

Being invited to a Japanese house for a meal is considered an honor. And being invited to spend the night is a rare honor, indeed. We were very flattered and pleased that the president of the Minaminhon Broadcasting Company, Suetaka Hatanaka, whose son attended Oglethorpe College, visited here many times. On one of his visits, he gave Atlanta's Botanical Gardens a stone lantern for its Bonsai garden.

At his home, we were privileged to enjoy a side of Japanese life that few visitors experience. The tranquility was intoxicating. The guesthouse in which we stayed was Japanese in style. I'll never forget waking up from a wonderful night's sleep, sliding open the shoji screen and experiencing early morning in his garden overlooking the sea. The guesthouse was attached to a French provincial villa. It was French in most details, including Mr. Hatanaka's splendid bed. His wife, however, preferred sleeping on the tatamis.

Throughout our stay, we found the Japanese proud of both their traditions and their cutting edge technology. They were eager to become more involved with global trade and were especially interested in learning about the advantages of establishing closer ties with Atlanta.

This trip became the catalyst for the opening of the Japanese Consulate in Atlanta. When the Japanese businessmen and politicians began coming to Atlanta to see if we really offered as much to them as we said, there was, of course, a lot of wining and dining; however, the two things that interested them most were baseball and golf. So, when we had a major VIP, we included a trip to Augusta to visit the famous National Golf Course and, if the time of year was April, they were fortunate enough to become part of the gallery at The Masters.

Once the Japanese opened a consulate here, they never had reason to regret it. It opened many doors for them and proved mutually beneficial for both countries and a province in Japan became associated with Georgia. The four-year rotation of Japanese consulates began, each staying his term then returning to Japan to assume another post.

The Japanese men, at that time, were not known for treating women as equals; however, they made me feel very important and were impressed that I had gone to the trouble to expand my knowledge of the Japanese language in preparation for their visit. Simple phrases, such as *thank you* and *please* in another person's native language can open many doors.

All the visitors brought gifts indigenous to their countries. The Japanese brought items that you might anticipate, such as vases, silk screens, and sake. The big surprise for most of us was the excellent quality of their Scotch.

Official visits such as these resulted in my being invited to other countries, including Germany, Austria, and South Africa.

Can Atlanta Go International?

The completion of Hartsfield International Airport in 1971 and the efforts of the Chamber's World Trade Council brought an ever increasing number of foreign visitors to Atlanta. The city itself had difficulty catching up with this new status. The following article appeared in the *Atlanta Journal and Constitution Magazine* in November, 1971.

When will Atlanta become an international city?

The day you can walk on Peachtree hearing several languages while no one turns around and stares in disbelief-

The day you can sip a Campari at an outdoor café on a balmy Sunday afternoon-

The day you can walk in a store and buy any item by exchanging your foreign currency-

The day you can land at Hartsfield International Airport without speaking one word of English, and find your way around without any problem-

The day you can open a local newspaper and find a whole page of international news-

The day you can watch an international ice-hockey game at the Coliseum while the Royal Danish Ballet plays at Symphony Hall-

The day you can ride a rapid transit vehicle and move about the city quickly and easily-

The day you can see flags of many nations flying in the breeze in front of hotels and other buildings-

That day you can say: Atlanta is an international city!

Why do I want Atlanta to become this international city? Simply because I will enjoy it more.

Like so many other European and Latin American wives, I came here not so long ago to find a small Southern provincial town. A foreign accent was like a disease and a foreign language was as rare as an elephant marching up Peachtree.

I recall the days when it was difficult to make myself understood in English with an accent. In order to buy what I wanted, I had to step behind the counter and point it out.

Today, Atlanta needs recognition from the world. Atlanta should take its place among the great cities of the continent. Atlanta strives to become the cosmopolitan city of the South. Yet today Atlanta is not an international city.

Atlanta has the potential to become such a city. How? By thinking international, as a starting point.

How do you think international?

Hop in a taxi and ask the driver to take you to the Restaurant *Rue de Paris*. If he doesn't wince and say, "How do you spell it?" he is thinking international.

If you order a Cinzano at a local restaurant and do not see dumb-founded expression on the waiter's face, he, is thinking international.

If you can buy a foreign newspaper at any newsstand, that is international.

An international mentality is one that accepts the concept of change, one that is familiar with "geography"; one that accepts different shades of skin; one that adjusts rapidly to different situations; one that can look at others with tolerance no matter what they wear, whether it is a sari or a Scottish kilt.

Thinking international comes from the exposure one has to the world outside our border: By inviting and welcoming here people from all nations, by providing international-style restaurants offering exotic foods, by supporting international festivals, sports events such as soccer, art groups with an international appeal.

Atlanta became a national city in the sixties. Only recently have our leaders, including the highest officials of the state and the city, taken a real interest in the potential of Atlanta as an international one.

Having traveled to many beautiful cities of the world, I am acutely aware of what is missing. We need more open spaces-beautiful parks and benches-broad avenues with large walking areas. Those who have walked through the Tivoli Gardens in Copenhagen and Champs Élysees in Paris, Promenade des Anglais in Nice, the Prater in Vienna, El Rosedal in Palermo, Buenos Aires, know what they would like to have here. The most popular and economical sport in Europe and Latin America is people-watching, and people moving about to see and be seen. This pastime accounts for countless outdoor cafes and restaurants.

We will need more information booths with multilingual services, at our airports, bus stations, stores, other public information areas. Often at a local hotel, a foreign visitor is stranded for lack of communication. At a bus station a woman sits on her suitcase and cries because she missed her bus and cannot make herself understood. More serious still, at a hospital's emergency room, a foreign patient is sick and cannot ask for the treatment he needs. We need the resources of the languages.

On the business front, foreign banks should be encouraged to locate here and bring their foreign staff and knowledge. Likewise foreign companies should be attracted here with a tax concession. Atlanta's 1,000-foot elevation and beautiful weather are not enough for a sales pitch.

Our educational system should assist in this transformation. Taxi and bus drivers, hotel, restaurant and store employees should be tuned in to the needs of the foreign visitor. Professional tour guides well versed in the local history would help. Policemen, telephone operators, Western Union clerks also need to be aware of the foreign influx. Our highway system needs to adopt the international symbols of communication – the first of which are just now being installed on the state's highways.

In the matter of protocol, we need to understand its importance to our foreign VIPS. Protocol is nothing but good manners and a certain accepted way of doing things universally. When we observe the rules of protocol we show due respect. We prove we are not insensitive and provincial. When we toast the head of a nation at an official banquet honoring a visiting ambassador, we show our *savoir faire*.

Atlanta desperately needs direct air routes to Europe and Latin America. At the present time Atlanta has only one international gate: Mexico City. Many people would come through Atlanta in order to avoid New York when going to Europe or coming back. It would be a pleasure to the third largest airport in the United States and be greeted with a peach. In Nice, they greet transatlantic passengers with a carnation.

In our quest for recognition, Atlanta should be represented at trade shows abroad, film festivals, tourist promotions, not only in English but in the language of the realm. Speak about Atlanta in Spanish, French, German. Praise Atlanta in Italian, Portuguese, Danish. It will reach the hearts of many people.

Convince the world that Atlanta is the place to visit in the immense Southeast, on a package tour. Coming here is very expensive for most foreign visitors; so once here they want to see as much as possible. We can help by including Atlanta on itineraries for package tours in this country and overseas. Our efforts should coincide with the airlines for maximum efficiency.

Our present image abroad is that of "Gone With the Wind." Let's change it to "Go With the Wind" at the same time we maintain our Southern Traditions and rich historical heritage that so delight the tourists.

Atlanta must encourage more and more career consulates general to locate here. Now only four career consulates general have offices here. We lag way behind Chicago with 59, New Orleans with 32, and Miami with 19. But in order to attract these foreign representatives and foreign companies here, we must offer a high quality of life with an international flavor.

As Atlanta acquires the many facets of a truly great city, foreign visitors will quickly recognize and appreciate them. Atlanta is willing. Atlanta will learn. This end cannot be achieved overnight. It will take patience, money, moral support and the same kind of spirit which has made Atlanta a famous national city.

The price we pay will be returned thousands of times. If we do our jobs well, the day will come when in a remote county on the other side of the world, someone will say: “Now, if there is one place I want to see before I die, it is the City of Atlanta.”

"Miss International"

Once a year the Chamber held an international dinner with a famous guest speaker, and my department was in charge of arranging for the speaker. The most famous of them was Robert Kennedy, who spoke to us not long after the assassination of his brother. I remember Robert Kennedy as an extraordinary personality with a presence that was entrancing. When you meet someone with this gift, you know you are standing before a great person.

As head of the Chamber's International Department, I became involved in history-making events. An exciting one was the 1971 rollout of Lockheed's C5-A. I stood there with all the congressmen and military officials, watching the plane taxi towards us. It was mammoth. To make certain, we would never forget the cargo carrier's size, when they opened the cargo doors, out drove four Greyhound buses. It was incredible; I couldn't believe it. But, on that occasion, we did not see the giant plane fly. They were afraid to risk it with so many important dignitaries standing there. If someone was hurt in any way, that could have been disastrous for the plane's future and the Atlanta area's economy. Lockheed was and remains one of Georgia's major employers.

I was involved in many events that marked major steps forward for the city. While I won't list them all, I cannot fail to mention a couple involving the importance of air travel and its role in Atlanta's growing prominence. Mayor William B. Hartsfield had laid the groundwork. Along with having been the driving force behind the construction of Atlanta's first two airports and having lured the FAA into establishing Atlanta as the southeastern hub for air traffic, instead of Birmingham, Hartsfield had dreamed of seeing Atlanta become an international terminal decades before it happened during a successor's administration.

To this day, Atlanta is not what I consider an international city. What it has is an international airport. However, a major step towards Atlanta becoming the international city it wants to be was the beginning of international flights out of Hartsfield Airport. Prior to 1971, going abroad to any country involved flying to a city with an international airport, such as Miami or New York, then transferring to another plane, often to another airline.

In the seventies, two airlines called Atlanta home: Delta and Southern Airways. But, it was Eastern Airlines that first connected Atlanta with the world. The first non-stop flight from Atlanta to a non-domestic destination departed for Mexico City June 25, 1971. I, working with Carolyn Wills, became the liaison between The Chamber, Eastern Airlines, Mayor Sam Massell, and the Mexican government, which earned my husband John's and my being included on the guest list for the trip. It was a great event, involving a full plane of executives and reporters. During the two full days of royal treatment in Mexico, we were wined and dined, taken to museums, to the Aztec ruins, and a performance by the country's national ballet troupe. Two weeks after our return to Atlanta, a delegation from Mexico flew to Atlanta, primarily leaders in education and business. We wined and dined them, took them to Stone Mountain and the limited number of other tourist attractions the city then had to offer.

The second international destination that could be reached non-stop from Atlanta was Kingston, Jamaica. An equal amount of pomp celebrated the linking of the two cities when the inaugural flight took place June 23, 1972. John and I made that trip, too, and had a wonderful time.

Country after country was eventually added to the short destination roster we began, for Atlanta, and soon the city was in need of a much larger air terminal. The opening of the new Hartsfield International Airport was in 1971. My most vivid memory of the opening day was an embarrassing glitch. All the computers that operated the trains and moving sidewalks were down; so we had to walk everywhere we went. And our tour took us from one side of the huge new airport to the other. Nonetheless, with the opening of the new facility, Hartsfield International moved steadily towards becoming the busiest air terminal in the U.S.

1972

Arab terrorist group Black September kills eleven Israeli athletes in the Olympic Village during the Munich Massacre. Prime Minister of Sweden Olaf Palme also uses the word massacre in describing the US bombing of Northern Vietnam. The US breaks all diplomatic ties with Sweden after Palme compares America to Nazi Germany. Though the government ceases contact with Sweden, President Nixon does establish economic relations with Chairman Mao Zedong on an eight day trip to Communist China, signs the SALT treaty with Brezhnev in Moscow, orders the development of the space shuttle program, and begins Vietnamization with the handover of the Long Binh military base to South Vietnam. All of this, and the fact that he increases Social Security spending by $5.3 billion, secures Nixon's presidency. But 1972 is also the year of the infamous June 17th Watergate break-in, which brings his incumbency to an abrupt end within a year.

A Day at the Farm with Governor Carter and President Figueres In Costa Rica

"Your young governor looks incredibly like the late John F. Kennedy," exclaimed Jose Figueres, president of Costa Rica. Governor Carter had just arrived at a dinner party in his honor at the home of our mutual friend, Juan Edgar Picado. Governor and Mrs. Carter were his house guests, and this evening the leaders of the country were assembled to meet them. It was an elegant gathering with black ties and long dresses. Spanish and English could be heard all through the room. The president continued, "He has the same youthful, dynamic look – truly a man of action – close to the people."

Governor Carter joined us, and Figueres repeated his statement. "You know, Governor, John F. Kennedy was much revered in Latin America. He was worshipped in Costa Rica. He gave hope to all of Latin America. In the humblest of homes you will find his portrait."

Carter replied, "I discovered the same thing throughout the other countries I have visited."

Earlier that day, we had met Governor and Mrs. Carter at the airport. The first storm of the rainy season was making its debut. While we waited for the plane to land, we could hear the thundering convulsion of the tempest.

The governor's host was having his own convulsion. With a distressed look on his face, Juan Edgar told me, "Rose, something has complicated my life. I thought everything was ready at the house to receive Governor and Mrs. Carter, and now! Would you believe that the plumbing in the guest room is acting up!

"A man came, took a look at the malfunction. He shrugged his shoulders and said *'No es nada'* (nothing to it). He then proceeded to separate the instrument into small pieces. An hour later, I looked in horror. The water closet was completely disassembled on the floor, and the plumber nowhere in sight!"

Juan Edgar continued, "I was furious. I called the plumbing company and asked for an explanation. The company insisted that they knew nothing about my problem and had not sent a man out. They said they had never heard of him. I was exasperated." Juan Edgar raised his hands up, *"¡Dios mio!* And the governor about to arrive!"

"What did you do, Juan Edgar?" I asked.

"Another plumbing company promised to send their most reliable man to make the repair."

Later that evening, Juan Edgar came over and whispered with relief, "the plumber walked out just as the governor walked in, and all is well."

At the reception, President and Mrs. Figueres stayed only a short time. However, the following day, my husband and I, along with the governor and his entourage, were to be guests at their farm, *La Lucha,* which is a two-hour ride from San Jose.

Governor Carter soon discovered that Figueres is, indeed, a unique president. Born in Costa Rica in 1906, of Spanish parents, he studied at the Massachusetts Institute of Technology. He is a farmer turned politician and a successful businessman, qualities he had in common with our governor. Figueres operates a 1,000-acre coffee and agave plantation and manufactures rope and coffee bags from the agave fiber.

Many recently criticized the President, better known as "Don Pepe," because he allowed the Soviets to open an embassy in San Jose, causing much concern in Costa Rica and Central America.

In a recent interview with The Wall Street Journal, Don Pepe explained that he did it to promote trade and ease the "cold war." The article pointed out that Don Pepe sees himself as a leader of a third-world force, in a new role as a Latin De Gaulle.

From 1940 to 1948, Costa Rica was ruled by a coalition of two different parties, both with communistic tendencies. They were well organized and tried to use force to obtain their objectives. When the 1949 elections took place, Otilio Ulate became president in a democratic election. Instead of accepting the election, the government abruptly ignored it and remained in power. It was a time of violence and unrest. Jose Figueres, together with several other men, set about to throw out the illegal government. It was then that he became a leader and a hero.

He is 5 foot 4, but his height in no way reduces his vitality. He is quick to give an opinion. He knows what he wants and goes after it. This directness and courage has made him a world figure and a popular president. He identifies with the average Costa Rican. According to The Wall Street Journal, Figueres describes himself as a "modern New Dealer who believes in social justice accomplished through a democratic system."

Following the civil war in 1948, Figueres became president but in 1949 stepped down. He turned the government over to Ulate who had been previously elected president for four years and again in 1970.

On our way to Don Pepe's farm, we planned to stop at the Volcano Irazu, the highest spot in Costa Rica – 11,000 feet above sea level. There, on a clear day, you can see half of Central America and both the Atlantic and Pacific Oceans.

We never made it to the summit. Word came through to the governor that there was an urgent call from Atlanta. We turned around, drove to Cartago, the town at the base of the volcano. Cartago was the first capital of Costa Rica but in 1910 was totally destroyed by an earthquake.

Rose and then Governor Jimmy Carter in Costa Rica

We stopped at a coffee plantation - Hacienda *El Molino* - where the governor placed his call to Atlanta.

He picked up the receiver with apprehension, and then I heard him sigh with relief and say, “I am happy with the action of the Supreme Court in regard to reapportionment. Please cancel the special session of the Legislature. May I take this opportunity to congratulate Attorney General Bolton and his staff on their excellent work?"

At the coffee plantation, the governor became very interested in its operation and decided to see the entire process. He asked, as he picked some coffee beans from an open sack, “How much does a coffee worker earn a month?”

“Two hundred thirty *colones* ($27),” replied the manager of the plantation. “The cost of coffee production is very expensive and because of the instability of the market, it is not to our advantage to concentrate on coffee as a major export.”

Later, we were to hear the same words expressed by President Figueres who strongly recommends diversified Costa Rican exports. An agreement with Russia is being studied whereby Russia would buy part of Costa Rica's surplus coffee if Costa Rica will spend one half the sales price for the purchase of equipment in Russia.

(Upon our return to Atlanta, Mrs. Carter mentioned to me that they had brought back a sack of green coffee beans. Now, she can roast, grind, and brew her own *café con leche,* Costa Rican style.)

In a statement to the press recently, Figueres said, "Aluminum could be our main export. It could be more than our coffee, bananas, and beef together." He announced that Alcoa had agreed to enter into a feasibility study with the Russians in regard to mining bauxite in Costa Rica.

The drive to Figueres' farm is breathtaking. Each curve on the road offers a different view. The flora and fauna along the road make it a naturalist's paradise. The mountains are covered with tropical growth, bananas, coffee and, agave.

The road is narrow and well paved but, by American standards, is dangerous. There is a lack of road fences and shoulders to inspire confidence. As our able driver of the Mercedes-Benz approached the farm, we could see the agave plant in abundance. It resembles the century plant that grows in Mexico.

Lucha Sin Fin, the name of Figueres' farm, means "battle without end," and this is both the philosophy and life of Figueres.

La Lucha is located in a valley 6,000 feet high. The main house is about 500 feet up the side of the mountain above the valley.

We were received in a guesthouse and were ushered into the living room and offered refreshments – beer, Cokes, and fruit juices.

Soon a small European car pulled up and the president and Mrs. Figueres got out. Figueres wore a beige *guayabera*, which is a sport shirt worn instead of a coat. Doña Karen was very chic in a navy blue pants suit with a white sweater. Both were very friendly and made everyone feel at ease.

The president speaks English fluently. He was pleasantly surprised to hear Governor Carter speak Spanish. The governor's Spanish is quite good. He gave a press conference entirely in Spanish to the amazement of the Costa Rican journalists. Although Doña Karen was born in New York City, she looks Scandinavian. Her blue eyes sparkle with vitality and intelligence. She is taller than the president and has a very dignified bearing. She wore her blond hair in a twist.

After lunch we gathered around the governor and the president in a very informal manner, lounging on the chairs and on the floor. The atmosphere was relaxed and casual and conducive to good conversation, and good conversation is exactly what happened. It was a rare experience to hear world events discussed by two people who had made history and were closely associated with world leaders.

Figueres turned to Carter and said, "The U.S. missed the boat when they did not elect Hubert Humphrey as President of the U.S.A. He would have been good for us and the world."

Hubert Humphrey admired Costa Rica and said once, "If every country in the world would follow the fine example of dedication to the principles of democracy exemplified by Costa Rica, this would be a world without war, a world without strife, and a world in which equality of opportunity and true freedom would be more than a promise. In fact, it would be a living reality."

Figueres continued, "I was with Adlai Stevenson on his visit to Latin America. He was a tremendous person. What a statesman. He was warmly received. Everyone liked him in Latin America."

"How about the Alliance for Progress program in Costa Rica?" asked Carter?

"A tremendous success," answered Figueres. "Every AID (Agency for International Development) program in Costa Rica was successful, helpful, and greatly appreciated. The U.S. AID program is generous, but it was a mistake to withdraw American support from the Aswan Dam in Egypt. John Foster Dulles, the late secretary of state, told me that was a calculated risk and insisted the U.S. get out of that aid program."

Figueres added, "Secretary of State Dulles and his policies were a complete failure in Latin America. He failed to understand the Latin mind."

The talk switched to the elections in the United States. Governor Carter said, "Ted Kennedy probably will run against Nixon. Humphrey is also running, and as a Democrat, I am cheering for my party." Carter added, "I will lead the Georgia Democratic delegation to the convention."

Jokingly, Figueres quipped: "I will run your campaign for you."

"Oh," said Carter, "I am not running for President this year." (And, of course, he later did and won.)

Then, the conversation turned to bananas and coffee. "As a major commodity," said Don Pepe, "coffee requires too much hand labor, and there is too much competition on the world market. We cannot complete with African countries that pay as little as 50 cents a day. We pay two dollars."

Carter commented, "We also have a labor imbalance with other countries."

Don Pepe continued, "We must diversify our exports. Do you realize that Costa Rica is more than 80 percent covered by forest? There is a real fortune here in lumber. Many different kinds of trees grow in Costa Rica."

He went on, pointing to the floor. "This floor is made of rosewood, very hard, heavy, and beautiful dark brown. A noble wood, like mahogany – too hard even to drive a nail into it."

"It requires no maintenance," added Doña Karen who was following the conversation with great attention.

"How about livestock?" asked Carter.

The President answered, "We have good cattle, and we have raised our cattle production and now export meat instead of importing it. The livestock industry is also one of our most promising businesses. There are several meat packing plants in Costa Rica, one operated by Armor.

"Costa Rica has a range of altitude which makes it possible to grow nearly every known subtropical fruit. Have you tasted our pineapple, mangos, and papayas? It is unfortunate that we have no apples and no peaches."

Doña Karen addressed the president as "Pepe" or sometimes as "honey." As the president talked about the experiment with apple trees, Doña Karen smiled and said, "Since Georgia is the famous Peach State, honey, tell the governor about your peaches."

Figueres smiled and said, "I would like to experiment with peach trees and apple trees." He pointed outside the window. "That's my only apple tree."

Doña Karen added laughingly, "It is better protected than the President." There is an eight-foot barbed-wire fence around the three-foot apple tree, and the tree has a serious case of fungus.

To this, Carter said, "Let me send you some Georgia apple and peach trees for your experiment."

Figueres replied, "Thank you, but I don't want just a few, I need at least a thousand, and I am willing to pay for them.

"Absolutely not," said Carter, "I will send them to you." He asked his aide to make a note to ask the commissioner of agriculture to follow up. "Perhaps someday I'll return here and taste some of your own home-grown apples and peaches."

While the governor and the president were discussing trees, Carter mentioned that he had brought the president something that he hopes will grow well in the fertile soil of Costa Rica. He then presented the president with a number of Georgia pine seedlings. Don Pepe was very moved and appreciative. Both he and Doña Karen exclaimed how nice and fresh they look. We shall plant them and hope to see them grow tall and strong."

Carter also brought with him an abstract oil painting, which he presented to Don Pepe, and to Mrs. Figueres a small, gold locket made from the famous Dahlonega gold.

Carter then explained to Figueres that Georgia was making progress but that Georgia was also an underdeveloped state compared to other states in the U.S.A. Figueres laughed and replied, "It would be progress for Costa Rica to be as underdeveloped as you are!"

As we were leaving, we were presented with colorful place mats of the same fiber produced on the farm. There were farewell hugs and the Latin American *"abrazo,"* and I felt that a strong tie of friendship was established between Jimmy Carter and Don José Figueres.

Later that evening in another reception for Governor and Mrs. Carter, we were treated to the grace and beauty of the Costa Rican folk dances. Suddenly, I felt myself believing that somehow the friendship developed in this people-to-people contact between the governor of the state of Georgia and the president of Costa Rica would be lasting. Even though the two men did not agree on everything, the personal contact developed in each an appreciation for the other's point of view. After all, this is what democracy and diplomacy are all about.

Jimmy Carter, Governor of Georgia
Rose Gold Cunningham — U.S. Ambassador to Costa Rica
José Figueres, President of Costa Rica — First Lady of Costa Rica, Karen Figueres

1973

President Richard Nixon ends wage price controls, and the Watergate scandal brakes, washing away his chances of completing his second term in office. Fighting brakes out between Arabs and Israelis, and Arab oil-producing nations move to embargo shipments of oil to the U.S., Japan, and Western Europe for supporting Israel. A fuel crisis ensues. The Greek monarchy is abolished by Premier George Papadopolous, who is quickly ousted in a bloodless coup that places General Phaedon Gizikis in power of what was once the cradle of democracy. The U.S. launches three space labs and Pioneer 10 transmits television pictures from close proximity of Jupiter. At the movies, the year's biggest hits are Woody Allen's *Sleeper* and *Last Tango in Paris*, starring Marlon Brando who also receives the Academy Award for his previous year's performance in *The Godfather*. And 1973 is the year I attend the most famous film festival of all.

Cannes Film Festival

In April 1973, my parents rented an apartment in Cannes, and I flew there to join them for a portion of their stay. Valerie, who was attending a private girls school in Switzerland, joined us for her spring break. One evening, she, my parents, and I drove to a restaurant in Beaulieu-sur-Mer. There, we met Charlie Chaplin, his wife, and two daughters. When they heard Valerie was attending a school in Switzerland, they promised to invite her to their house, which they said was not far away. They never did. That night, we, also, saw the bizarre Spanish painter, Salvador Dali.

At the beach, on seeing a group of prostitutes, Papa asked Mama if she minded if he inquired what their rate was, since the dollar had gone down in value. "Sure, go and ask," she said with a laugh.

And, he did. From afar, we saw one of the prostitutes hit him with her bag. That sent him running back to Mama and me to report, "The rate is a hundred dollars an hour. I told her that it takes me an hour to take my shoes off." To that Mama replied, "You should wear your house shoes."

Cannes had more than its usual share of famous faces during our visit. On my flight over, Elizabeth Taylor was among the passengers and was met by Richard Burton when she landed. They were on their way to the 26th International Cannes Film Festival, and I became determined to find a way to attend the opening ceremony of this internationally famous annual event. The only way for me to do that was to find some way by which I could become an insider.

After Valerie returned to school, the city began feverishly getting ready for the festivities. Hundreds of large flags representing many countries bordered the main artery and flew in the breeze. Most stores listed the current rate of foreign exchange in their windows, multilingual signs of welcome were permanently and prominently displayed at major points of interest, and by pressing a button to choose the language of your choice, you heard the recorded explanation of the landmarks you visited. The presence of so many nationalities gave me an idea, and I headed for the Festival's headquarters in the Carlton Hotel.

The place was brimming with fresh flowers, potted plants, and huge posters that advertised movies, while outside, the Bentleys were in full force. Once inside, I headed for the Film Festival's main desk. I told the woman on duty that I wanted to serve as an interpreter and asked where I could register. In response, I encountered nothing but typical French negativism. Even though I made it clear that I spoke multiple languages and was there to offer, free of charge, my services as an interpreter to anyone who might need one, I was met with total indifference. According to the woman at the desk, they were not set up to even put up a notice regarding the availability of translation services because "All the attendees bring their own interpreters. Everyone."

I quickly learned this was not completely accurate. A man who had overheard the conversation came over and asked if he could speak with me? I said, "Certainly," and he introduced himself as Baruch Dienar, a motion picture producer from Israel. He was a Sabra, one born in Israel, and a handsome one at that: tall, in his mid-fifties with piercing brown eyes. To my surprise, the first question he asked me was: "Are you a terrorist?"

It was hard not to laugh, as I asked him, "Do I look like one?"

Furthermore, I can't imagine a real terrorist answering such a question truthfully. Perhaps it was the look on my face that passed the test. After saying that I was merely an interpreter from the United States who happened to be in Cannes on holiday, he wanted to know if, by any chance, Romanian was one of my languages. When, to his surprise, I said that it was, he was delighted. "Wonderful! Let's talk."

He told me that Romania was a major market for his films and that he would be holding a screening for some distributors from Romania. For the occasion and in preparation for it, he needed an adept translator to assist in issuing invitations and with the negotiations that would follow the preview. When I said that I would be delighted to help him, he quickly asked what I would charge. I told him that my services were free – if he could acquire passes for my parents and me to attend the opening ceremonies. Unfortunately, Valerie could not attend, as she had to return to school. Baruch said that would be no problem and, good as his word, he did get us three of the highly coveted tickets.

To earn our tickets, I first had to be officially recognized as the interpreter for Baruch Dienar Productions of Israel. I went with Baruch to have our pictures taken for our credentials. Both his picture and mine looked like hell, but they were glued to identification cards and officially encased in plastic. That was all that mattered; that card became my master key. It gave me passage to virtually anywhere I chose to go. Once I had the all-important card, my job was to contact the distributors and the press to tell them about Dienar's movie and invite them to the preview. Special attention was given to the Romanian delegation, and they showed up in force for the screening.

Over the next few days prior to the screening, I mastered a whole new vocabulary, the film industry's terms for everything. It was like learning a sixth language, one spoken in a strange and exciting world.

At first, I was concerned that I might not have packed the right wardrobe for my involvement with the Festival, but I soon learned that clothes were not an issue. Except for the opening ceremonies, the official dress in town seemed to be jeans (both blue and white). On the beach, it was bikinis, with the starlets in topless monokinis. It was a world of show business, big business, dirty business that attracted some of the nicest people and some of the scum.

The Carlton and the streets of Cannes swarmed with odd characters, gays, lesbians, phonies, buyers, sellers, and the press, which had to be wined and dined, courted and coddled. A director depends on the distributor, and the distributor depends on the press. It was important for Baruch that there were no weak links in the chain.

When I arrived at the theater where his screening was to take place, I found that the police heavily guarded it. While there was a great deal of security visible at all the Festival venue, this screening seemed to have far more than I saw elsewhere. Even in 1972, the Jews were always afraid of encountering terrorists wherever they went.

Once seated inside the theater, I, along with the press and distributors from around the world, saw the preview of Baruch's film *Take Two*. It was a human-interest story that was highly seasoned with sexually explicit scenes, certainly more than one saw in American films of that time. The negotiations seemed to go well, and Baruch was pleased with the results and my contribution to them. Again, I found that the way to truly enjoy any event is to be a participant, rather than merely a spectator.

During the weeklong Festival, my parents and I saw several of the films that other producers and stars were there to promote. But, a little bonus I received from Baruch has always been the real highlight of the experience for me. He told me that my name in Hebrew is *Soshana*, and I think it's beautiful.

The day of the opening ceremonies, I was at the Carlton Hotel in order to go over schedule and plans with Baruch Dienar. When I stepped into an elevator, I found myself face to face with a childhood idol, Ingrid Bergman, who was regally dressed in an ivory brocade dress; however, she looked very tired. Bergman was president of the Festival that year, and was there with her son in order to preside over the opening ceremonies. I introduced myself to her and

Signed photograph of Ingrid Bergman

said that when I was a teenager, I had written her a letter, to which she had kindly replied by sending me an autographed photograph. "I still have the photo and consider it a cherished keepsake," I told her.

She seemed quite touched, was most gracious, and shook my hand before we went our separate ways. It was later that I learned she had cancer, which took her life shortly after she completed her last movie. In it, she played Golda Maier, Prime Minister of Israel.

The evening of the opening ceremonies, Bergman looked radiant and beautiful. And, frankly, so did my parents and I. We donned our formal finery for the festivities and spent a memorable evening among the international galaxy of stars that had come to see and be seen.

My father's distinguished and elegant presence got him mistaken for a producer by more than one person who came over to meet him.

1975

Powerful members of the Nixon Administration are convicted and sentenced for the Watergate cover-up. U.S. cuts off aid to Turkey, fierce fighting erupts between Ethiopian government troops and secessionist guerrillas, King Faisal of Saudi Arabia is assassinated by a nephew who, in turn is beheaded, and U.S. withdraws its last combat aircraft from Taiwan. Bloody religious fights break out in Beirut, while leaders of 35 nations sign the Helsinki accord, and Portugal grants independence to its African colonies. Richard Adams' *Watership Down* and Robert Stone's *Dog Soldiers* draw booklovers, while Edward Albee's *Seascape* and Ed Bullins' *The Taking of Miss Jean Brodie* sweep live theater prizes. The Episcopal priesthood welcomes women to its ranks, Pope Paul VI canonizes five saints, and New York City's Council of Churches denies membership to Sun Myung Moon's Unification Church. *Jaws, Nashville,* and *The Sunshine Boys* are movie blockbusters, and Beverly Sills wins the heart of opera fans, and *A Chorus Line* begins its phenomenal Broadway run. U.S. and Soviet spacecrafts link in space, and the U.S. Viking begins its unmanned journey to Mars for signs of life. U.S. unemployment reaches a post-war high of 9.2 %, Teamster president, James Hoffa, "disappears," Mauna Loa erupts in Hawaii for the first time in 15 years, and the U.S. marks the start of the American Revolution Bicentennial with ceremonies at Boston's Old North Church.

The South African Adventure

When I traveled to South Africa in 1975, during the days of Apartheid, their government leaders felt that the international press was bias. Considering me an opinion former because of my position at the Chamber, I was invited to see Apartheid's segregation policies in action and judge for myself whether or not their people would benefit from immediate integration.

During my three-week stay, I learned what a complex, multi-cultural country South Africa was and the difficulties the government faced in creating an across-the-boards educational standard. Their national flower, the Prometheus, grows in forty different varieties with a rainbow of colors; their racial profile was equally complex. In addition to the blacks (multiple tribes who were collectively known as Bantus) and the Coloureds (those of mixed blood), there were also people from Holland (known as Afrikaaners), Great Britain and India. The Bantus were in no way united; each tribe despising the next, and all seemed to stay on the brink of war. The non-blacks were also divided into groups by nationality, especially the Indian community, which had brought its rigidly held cast system with it to South Africa.

In the 70's, according to Allen Drury's aptly named book, *A Very Strange Society*, there were 3.5 million Afrikaaners and white English, 1.5 million Coloureds, who descended from Whites, Bushmen, Hottentots and Malaysian, 0.5 million Asians (mostly Indians), and 12.5 million Bantus, which included seven major ethnic groups: the Zulus, the Ciskey, the Xhosa, the Sotho, the Tswana, the Bapedi, and the Shangaan, as well as some minor tribes.

Each national faction had its own representative that went to South Africa's capital, Pretoria, to voice his or her people's concerns. Without exception, these spokespersons were the best educated within each group. I particularly remember a meeting in Natal with two representatives of the Indians, very formal gentlemen. Each introduced himself with the inclusion of his religious affiliation. One introduced himself as Moslem, the other as Hindu. Feeling a need to lighten matters up, I introduced myself as Jewish. My sense of humor failed to reach them, and both clammed up, making it the only nonproductive and uninformative meeting during my visit.

I, of course, met with leaders in the black community. Of particular interest was the Xhosa tribe, whose tribal language included a clicking sound they made with their tongue when speaking. An interview that I especially remember was with an extremely liberal woman who lived in Soweto, the black township outside of Johannesburg. The lady was adamant that the white controlled government had to go, which it eventually did, in 1994.

One of the issues that I felt she chose not to acknowledge was that the black tribes did not get along and were continually at odds with one another. It was the white government in power that held the tribes together and generated a measure of cooperation among them.

As my travels took me over the entire country, my biggest shock and disappointment was learning that the black children were not offered educational opportunities, only the Europeans and Indians. The explanation I received was that the government could not afford to school the vast number of black youngsters.

Some of the whites admitted that they feared for their lives when they eventually, and inevitably, lost control of the government. They had good reason for concern because a shift from white control of government to black in neighboring countries had been accompanied by massacres of whites. Fortunately, when South Africa's government later became black controlled, it happened with a minimum amount of out revolt or revolt and slaughter.

One stop on my tour was a game preserve, where some French VIPs invited me to join them to watch what was called a lion kill. What we were supposed to see was the lions feeding on wild impalas. The people at the reserve considered watching the lions capturing and devouring their prey a great show. I found it a gruesome site, especially when two of the male lions decided to fight to the death over some of the prey served up for them. That night, I didn't have much appetite for dinner. They served grilled impala.

On other occasions, I frequently dined on the country's fantastic lobster and greatly enjoyed their excellent wines. As in England, the popular drink was tea, and like in England, they eat with their left hand and drive on the left hand side of the road. One of the euphemisms I quickly became familiar with was "Do you need to spend a penny?" which translates *do you need to go to the bathroom?*

Travel accommodations, like their bathrooms, in South Africa, ranged from Spartan to absolute luxury. The government invited me to ride what was known as *The Blue Train*, a train on which you were expected to dress formally for dinner. During the trip, I became acquainted with an executive from the BBC. At that time, there was only radio in South Africa; however, he was there to initiate television broadcasting. That same year, 1975, television made its debut in South Africa.

The famous South Africa diamond mines, in Kimberley, were a stop on the rail portion of my tour. When we exited the train to look around, I took a picture of a man in chains. And, here came the police, saying it was illegal to photograph a felon. Even though I explained that I had been given carte blanche to photograph whatever I pleased, they insisted on removing the film from my camera and destroying it.

In Umtata, I had the opportunity of visiting members of the Xhosa Development Corporation, the pride and joy of a newly formed country but still under the leadership of the white government.

I also traveled by private air charter in a 15-passenger plane that flew low so we could see the antelopes running across the land below. What a sight!

Interviewing people was new to me, and before I gave it a try, I was frankly terrified of the task ahead. I discovered, however, that I have a knack for asking the right questions. One of my interviews was with a Member of Parliament, Helen Suzman. She was an extremely liberal person who felt segregation in South Africa must immediately end. In passing, she mentioned that her nephew had moved from South Africa to Atlanta, Georgia.

Perhaps the most memorable experience came as a result of having no plans one evening. My escort in Cape Town, Rose Du Toit, was a widow whose husband had been a cardiologist. She called to ask if, on my evening off, I would like to accompany her to dinner at a friend's house. It was not until I was in her car and on my way that I learned our destination was the home of the famous heart surgeon, Dr. Christian Barnard, the man who made the first heart transplant. Rose Du Toit's husband, I learned, had been on Dr. Barnard's highly revered team.

He and his beautiful young wife of 23, Barbara, lived in a gorgeous house overlooking the ocean at Cape Town. At the time, they had a child on the way, as well as one age three and another age one-and-a-half.

Present also for the dinner party were Barbara Barnard's German parents, wealthy industrialists then living in Argentina. I disliked them immediately, knowing that they were Nazi sympathizers. But, of course, I tried to keep a civil tongue and focused my attention on the others present.

When Dr. Barnard heard that I was born in Romania, he explained with glee that he had recently returned from Bucharest, where he had performed a very difficult heart operation on a six-year-old boy, saving his life.

Christian Barnard was an imposing figure, clear blue eyes, six feet two inches tall and all muscle. The man carried himself with authority and loved to talk about his friendships with politicians, shahs, sheiks, and actors such as Peter Sellers, Gina Lollobrigida, Audrey Hepburn, and Richard Burton. He had a lot of names to drop.

When arthritis progressed to the point he could no longer perform heart surgery, he moved to Switzerland, where he opened a face lifting and rejuvenation institute. Dr. Barnard died in 2002.

At the conclusion of my three-week visit to South Africa, I did form some opinions. First and foremost, the Republic of South Africa had every complex and difficult situation a government could have. It was and still is a tribal society divided into numerous clans. When the Republic was formed, its entire people had the same basic opportunities. There was ample land for anyone willing to clear and farm it. The Afrikaaners applied themselves with diligence, discipline, determination and skill.

The Bantus came down from the north and had the same work opportunities. They, however, did not apply themselves. All of these black clans hate each other. Instead of building a productive society, they were satisfied with petty wars against one another. Like other countries pulling away from ethnic injustice, Only education and time will help South Africa. But nothing – absolutely nothing – rationalizes the injustice of the white-imposed Apartheid System.

That said, I am still not certain that South Africa has really benefited from its sudden abandonment of segregation, prior to raising the educational standards of some of its factions. Education should have come first. The country is now suffering from the ravages of AIDS, teamed with uncontrolled prostitution. Furthermore, the country's brightest and best minds have moved to other countries, creating a tragic brain drain that has left South Africa poor in the most devastating way poorer than it was before. It is education that is the great divider of people. Knowledgeable people with long-range plans for progress and improvement must run Republics and democracies. These are essentials that South Africa now seems to lack.

It's unavoidable comparing the segregated South Africa of 1975 with Atlanta prior to integration. When I traveled to South Africa, Atlanta's public schools had been integrated for 15 years, and public facilities had been integrated some years before. I think this surprised some of our visitors. When the black Prime Minister of Jamaica came to visit, he was just another visitor to the Commerce Club receiving VIP treatment. If he had arrived, say, ten years earlier, that would have been a different story.

Divorce and Tony

As mentioned earlier, I traveled to South Africa. The year was 1975, and a great many important events in my life were connected with that journey, some professional, others personal. As a result of my profession, a representative of the Government of South Africa came to my office at the Chamber and handed me an invitation for John and me to travel to South Africa as guests of the country. "Why me?" I asked the representative.

"You are an opinion former," he answered.

When I got home that evening, a new personal chapter began, as well. As I ran up the steps and rushed into the house, I could hardly contain my excitement as I showed the invitation to John. He took one look and said, "I'm not going."

"But, John, it's first class travel all the way. It's the opportunity of a lifetime."

"I said, I'm NOT going. And, neither are YOU." His voice was filled with anger, and soon mine was, too.

"Oh yes, I AM going."

"If you do, it will be as a divorced woman."

I was furious. At the time, things were not going well between John and me, and this became the final straw. The next day, he spoke with his attorney and started the divorce proceedings. I left all the terms of the divorce up to John and the attorney. Some were strange, indeed. John would not move out of the house; he would merely move to the ground floor and live in what had been his old office space and the maid's room, while the girls, now 15 and 17, and I would continue living upstairs. The routine of the household would not change. John would even continue having meals with the family. Those were his terms, and I, somewhat to my surprise, had no problem with them.

Two days before I departed alone on the splendid trip, the divorce was final. So, in a strange sort of way, both of us got the conditions we demanded. I would go to South Africa (my demand), but I would go as a divorced woman (John's demand). On my return from South Africa, we lived under the conditions he set forth in the divorce agreement for more than two years; however, there were major changes in my personal life.

Shortly before I left, a casual acquaintance (whom we will call Tony) stopped by the Chamber on business. Tony was high in the ranks of a major corporation that had extensive business interests in Europe; so, he often traveled back and forth to his native England and around Europe. In the course of conversation during coffee break at a meeting, he learned about my trip and that I planned short stays in England and France on my way back to the U.S. When he heard this, he asked the date I would arrive in London? I told him and was surprised to learn that he would be there at that time. "Why don't you let me show you my city?" he asked.

The prospect of an escort with entrée to places off limits to even an honorary consul sounded very appealing. The understanding was that the relationship was that of two unattached old friends, nothing more. After all, we had known one another for twelve years and were frequently at the same business and social events in Atlanta. In fact, the plan was for our Great Britain travels to be chaperoned, so to speak, by friends of his, a couple who lived outside of London. We were even invited to stay at their home and accepted their invitation. That was the plan, but it didn't work out that way. Romance began.

Perhaps Tony had ideas and plans all along, but I truly didn't. I was just getting a taste of being single, something that I had denied myself when I was young. Becoming immediately involved in an on-going relationship was not what I had envisioned or thought that I wanted. But, my plans were definitely changed by this persuasive and appealing man. I quickly became fascinated with this tall, blue-eyed, silver-haired man's flair for living and undeniable charm.

We became lovers. Passionate lovers. The physical thrill of the relationship far exceeded even my affair with Grant. I call the next two years a sabbatical of love. Tony knew all the intricacies of lovemaking. He taught me how to respond, how to enjoy each caress, until he knew more about my body than I did.

When we returned to Atlanta, I told my parents about the new love interest in my life. Mama was not thrilled. She had met Tony at many social functions, and subsequent meetings did not change her opinion. "He's just a playboy," was her summation. And, in retrospect, I have to say that she was right.

While Tony was the perfect person to party with and the perfect sexual partner, he was not someone on whom you could depend. Over the next two-and-a-half years, I became progressively aware of his weaknesses and failings. As tempting as his proposals of marriage were on social and romantic levels, I could not shake my reservations. Perhaps there were more feelings within me that I was not acknowledging.

During my divorce, Tony never came to the house. That, I did not permit because I would never have done that to John. I saw no reason to further hurt him or involve the girls. While all of them had met Tony long before I left for South Africa, none of them were eager to see the two of us together.

My mother repeatedly told me to have my fun but not to look on Tony as marriage material. His business success did not budge her from her appraisal of him nor the fact that he asked me on more than one occasion to leave the girls with John and marry him.

Two-and-a-half years into our relationship, I was dealing with a crisis with one of my teenage daughters. When I tried to talk to Tony about the situation and get his input, he merely shrugged his shoulders and said, "That's your problem."

His response made me see him as Mama did, as someone who wanted all the fun of a relationship without any of the problems. I could clearly see the mistake I would be making in marrying him and broke off the relationship.

John had not lived the life of a hermit, following the divorce. While his foremost interests were his architectural work and the children, he had been dating a Japanese girl. Nonetheless, I knew that he was still very much in love with me. And, I finally admitted to myself that I was still very much in love with him. Despite our faults, we both cared for one another deeply.

One day I decided to talk to him about getting back together, and we quickly came to terms and agreed to a second marriage, which would be on the date of our first marriage in Cuba. On December 23, 1979 we remarried with our daughters as our witnesses. In order to be present, our girls, who had Christmas jobs at an Atlanta department store, asked to be excused from work to attend their parents' wedding. The store's management was most accommodating, and we were once again a whole family.

It took me years to recognize the secret reservoirs of John's determination. Here was a man who had flown fifty combat missions, a man who was decorated seven times with the air medal, twice for good conduct. Furthermore, he had received two Presidential Citations. He is a man who had the discipline to study and graduate from a tough and respected school, Georgia Tech, to become a recognized architect and a specialist in his field. John had come from a humble background – yet he lifted himself to commendable heights. Through bravery, character, tenacity, courage and hard work he overcame having no money or connections to start his own firm, little by little, guiding it to success and recognition.

I admire his tenacity and respect his dedication to his work and to what he believes. The esteem I hold for him has grown into a mature and deep-rooted love. While we still see the world from different angles and will never place identical values on what life offers, I clearly see how important he is to me and how much I appreciate having him as part of my life.

Leaving the Chamber

During my decade with the Chamber, a lot of things happened because I made them happen. I must say I was great at my job and loved it. Every day was different and exciting, but good things sometimes come to an abrupt end. That was true for me and for my boss. In spite of his extraordinary track record, Opie Shelton was fired. His was a politically appointed position, and by 1975, Opie's supporters were no longer in power.

His replacement was a country boy who didn't even know how to spell *international*, much less know the finer points of protocol. It probably isn't surprising that he and I did not see eye to eye. One day during the visit of a Japanese delegation, the new man immediately started treating them like a bunch of good ol' boys, throwing his arms around them and slapping their backs. After the delegation left, I took the new manager aside and told him that you must never touch the Japanese. This made him very angry. "Are you calling me a queer?" he demanded.

"Not at all," I said. "What I'm saying is in the Japanese culture they do not like to be touched. That's why they bow. You can talk to them, but you cannot so much as shake hands. That's not part of their culture."

My new boss was not in the habit of taking advice – especially from a woman. Within three months, he fired me, saying that he wanted to get someone better versed in international experience. Furthermore, he wanted a man. Well, he got a man, but I'm not convinced that the new head of The International Department filled the other qualification.

When NOW, the National Organization of Women, found out what had happened to me, they urged me to sue the Chamber for discrimination and asked me to come see them. When I met these shabby-looking women in their dreadful offices, I decided I didn't want to have anything to do with their organization, nor did I want to burn all my bridges. I accepted my defeat and went home – but not for long.

"Latin Atlanta" and Bill

In 1975, still smarting over the loss of my position at the Atlanta Chamber, I looked about for a new opportunity to create an interesting job for myself. It occurred to me that the local public television station might be where I should turn.

I made an appointment with Danny Royal, the producer at WABE-TV, which was the city-owned Atlanta Public Broadcasting System affiliate. The idea I presented him was producing a weekly talk show in Spanish, with me as anchor, of course. At the time, there was not the sizeable Latin population that Atlanta has today, and they were largely ignored by the entire city. Only one grocery store stocked the items essential to various forms of Latin cuisine and no other businesses seemed interested in tapping into this small – but growing – market. I felt that Atlanta's Latin population deserved at least 30 minutes of television each week in their native language.

In spite of the fact that I had zero on-camera experience, Danny thought my idea of a talk show in Spanish with all Spanish-speaking guests had possibilities and said that he would approve the taping of a pilot program. After seeing it, he would make his final decision. Before I left, other basics were spelled out for me. The show's budget was nearly non-existent; I would receive fifty dollars per show, as my fee. For that princely sum, I would have to be both producer and anchor. There would be no budget for guests, transportation of guests, or incidentals. If someone needed a cab to get to the station, I had to pick him/her up or pay the cabbie out of my pocket. In spite of the less than attractive conditions, I saw that the series *Latin Atlanta* was another frontier for me and worth my time. Danny found an open taping slot on the station's busy schedule.

Having no particular guest in mind for this all-important one shot at having my own series, I contacted Atlanta Council for International Visitors and learned that a city planner from Lima, a Mr. Pedro Gonzalez, would be arriving in town the day we were to tape the pilot show. He was the guest of the State Department, and his visit was to be a high-profile event. After a stop in Dallas, he was continuing to Atlanta. Contacts were made and details were ironed out. I was to meet Mr. Gonzalez at the airport and bring him straight to the television station for the taping. When I told Danny what I had arranged, he was clearly impressed. I then hit the books, studying the Encyclopedia and everything else I could find about his country and city planning.

On the appointed day, I went to the airport a bit early, anxious for everything to go well. Mr. Gonzalez was due to arrive on an Eastern Flight; so, to pass the time while waiting, I struck up a conversation with an Eastern employee I knew named Mario. He happened to be the only Spanish speaking gate agent in the entire airport. Mario and I chatted a bit while I waited for the flight from Dallas.

Much to my relief, Mr. Gonzalez's flight was on time – but no Mr. Gonzalez deplaned. There I stood, empty-handed. I wandered around the airport frustrated and dejected. No guest meant no pilot program; no program meant no television series; no series meant no career in television. I had to do something – but what?

Suddenly, I remembered Mario and tracked him down. "How would you like to be on TV? It would be a great exposure for Eastern Airlines."

"Well … I guess so," he replied. "I'll see if I can get approval. When would you like to do it?"

"Now!" I practically shouted. "Now. We leave for the television station now. We can rehearse in the car on the way there."

"No, no, no," he protested, gesticulating in the Latin habit. "I'm not ready, I'm not ready!"

"It's now or never. Get your supervisor's permission and let's be on our way."

Not at all certain he should, Mario kept mumbling, "But, I'm not ready," as he went to his supervisor, explained what I was proposing. To Mario's dismay, the supervisor gave his approval and agreed to have someone cover for Mario while he was gone. With that, we were on our way to the parking lot. As I drove to the station, Mario continued protesting that he had nothing of interest to offer. "We'll talk about your career, about your family," I said. "Don't worry, everything will go just great." I did my very best to believe that.

I arrived at the station with a reluctant guest who kept saying, "But I'm not ready." Neither was I. I had zero experience in following the floor manager's cues concerning which camera to speak directly to, what all the little hand signals meant, and not a clue as to how long 30 minutes can seem when cameras are staring at you.

Quiet in the studio! Rolling tape. Five … four … three." One at a time, the floor manager folded the two remaining fingers he held in the air, pointed at me, and, we were on. I talked to Mario about his job, how he came to be an Eastern employee, his family, his likes, and his dislikes. Soon, he was the relaxed one, and I was the one battling stage freight. The last three minutes of the pilot show were the longest three of my life. After exhausting the subject of his career, I asked whatever came to mind. Where do you shop for groceries? What is your favorite food? Your favorite toothpaste? Your dog's name? We laughed a lot, I asked crazy questions, and Mario answered them all.

After the taping, I was in a daze when Danny came out of the control room and announced, "You're hired, Rose. I don't speak a word of Spanish and have no idea what you two were talking about, but you two laughed a lot and seemed to be having such a great time, I know there's an audience for your show."

That's how I started my career as a TV anchor.

The next day, Mr. Gonzalez called from the Biltmore Hotel, apologizing for having missed his plane. He said he would be delighted to still do the interview, if I was interested. I quickly called Danny and asked if we could tape another show, since the opportunity had presented itself. He agreed, and I immediately called Mr. Gonzalez back to say that I would be waiting in front of the Biltmore for him in twenty minutes.

When I reached the hotel, on the sidewalk a gentleman stood waiting. I rolled down the car window and asked in Spanish, "Are you Mr. Pedro Gonzalez?"

"Sí, that's my name."

"*Por favor*, get into the car. We'll go straight to the station."

Although he seemed a bit uncertain whether or not it was what he wanted to do, he climbed in, and we were on our way. However, it was soon apparent to both of us that our conversation was not making any sense. He claimed not to know what "station" I meant or to have any recollection of speaking to me on the phone. No wonder! This Pedro Gonzalez was an encyclopedia salesman from Puerto Rico who was in town to attend a convention. In retrospect, I know that the name Pedro Gonzalez is as common in the Spanish-speaking world as John Smith is in the English-speaking world. Still, the odds of two men with the same Spanish name being registered at the same hotel on the same day are not something you might expect at that time in Atlanta.

I arrived at the station, with the encyclopedia salesman, not quite knowing what to do with him. Mercifully, a call was waiting for me, a call from the city planner, Gonzalez. I practically begged him to take a cab to the TV station, assuring him I would be waiting to pay the fare.

I interviewed both the salesman and the city planner. It proved to be an interesting show – perhaps not always as much fun as my interview with Mario – yet, it was good television with a strong appeal to Atlanta's Hispanic community.

Latin Atlanta had a successful run which ended because of budget cuts. Nonetheless, I proved that my idea for an all-Latin show met a need in the marketplace and interviewed an interesting array of the famous and not so famous. Without question, my favorite guest was William F. Buckley, Jr. - a man I discovered is simply full of surprises, including the fact that he speaks fluent Spanish.

The following account tells how we met, but it doesn't include how I became lucky enough to have him as a guest on *Latin Atlanta*. Before his arrival in Atlanta, I called to ask Buckley if he would be a guest on my show. He said that I would need to contact his agent and that his fee was ten thousand per appearance. I laughed and said that I would pay him half my fee for doing the show. "What do they pay you?" he asked. When I told him fifty dollars, he laughed and said that he would accept those terms only if I would allow him to take me to lunch before the taping.

Bill Buckley and Rose taping *Latin Atlanta.*

The show with William F. Buckley, Jr. as my guest and the dinner described in the following article led to a friendship and correspondence that continues to this day. When he and John met, they hit it off immediately, both having such similar political views. Over the years, we've remained friends and correspond from time to time. My letters in Spanish are answered in English. His writing skills in Spanish are not as developed as his ability to speak the language. I've also built a collection of Bill's books. Most are signed, first editions that he's either sent to or delivered to me personally.

Guess Who's Coming To Dinner

"Guess who's coming to dinner?" I yelled to John through the closed bathroom door, "WILLIAM F. BUCKLEY, JR.!"

I heard a great splash and a gasp. I thought John was drowning.

It all started when I read in the paper that Buckley was scheduled in Atlanta in about three days for one of those high-priced speaking engagements. Gus, our Belgian friend who has known Buckley for many years, and I, decided to write Buckley and invite him to have dinner with us while in town. "Gus just called," I told John, "and read me Buckley's fax. *'If invitation still open, I accept.'* "

My admiration for Buckley dates back several years. I don't always agree with his political views, but I am intrigued with his cleverness when debating an opponent on television. His raised eyebrows, his triumphant leer, his arrogant tone, and the way he flicks his tongue like a snake about to strike. And strike he does!

His interesting background also captivates me. His family reminds me much of the Kennedys and their talents, ambition, and accomplishments. His is a close-knit family of ten children born of William F. Buckley and Aloise Steiner, who are big news in their own rights. A multi-millionaire, the senior Buckley believed in educating his children above everything else. All of his girls write. Priscilla, the only unmarried one, is managing editor of *National Review*, the most conservative weekly publication in the USA.

I had read that William F. Buckley, Jr. likes French food and that his lovely wife Pat is an excellent cook and can cope with 29 dinner guests when her husband has told her there would only be 20.

Gus, his wife Mariette, and I met the plane from Miami, where Buckley had spoken to a group of broadcasters. (John didn't come; he was home cooking.) Before the plane arrived, Gus remarked, "Wonder how much luggage he has?"

"For such a short stay, probably only one overnight bag," I guessed.

Not only did he carry an overnight bag; he also had two large briefcases, one portable typewriter, and a huge, bulky folding suitcase. Watching Buckley, at 6'2", and Gus, at 5'2" struggle to wedge all that luggage into my little car was a comical sight.

"Buckle up, Mr. Buckley," I said as we climbed into my Chevrolet. "Your life is now in the hands of a crazy French woman driver."

"Call me Bill," he smiled.

"Muy bien, Guillermo," I replied in Spanish.

"Where did you learn to speak Spanish?" he asked.

"I lived in Havana six years BC … Before Castro," I said.

Bill told me he had learned Spanish in Mexico and Venezuela, where his father had started an oil business.

Gus broke in with a few well-chosen phrases in French and Bill quickly replied in fluent French.

"And where did you learn French?" I asked, impressed.

"I learned it in France," he said simply, "but I don't speak it well."

I had to disagree.

It was great fun. All evening we jumped back and forth from English to French to Spanish and back to English. Bill remarked that he had to speak Spanish frequently; his housekeeper doesn't speak English.

"We have the same situation at our house," I said. "My Costa Rican friend, Anita, doesn't speak English. So, we jabber in Spanish – and John keeps guessing what we're saying."

"The last time I was in Atlanta, I stayed in that hotel with the hole in the center," said Buckley with a laugh.

"Well, this time you're staying at the one with the holes all around it," I said.

I had to stop to buy hamburgers for my daughter, Marcelle, because of our late dinnertime.

"Let me get them," Bill offered, climbing out.

I watched him stride jauntily into the burger joint. Mr. William F. Buckley, Jr. - author, political candidate, most widely syndicated political columnist in the country, editor-in-chief of his own *National Review*, renowned lecturer, director, star of his own television show *Firing Line*, and who knows what other accomplishments - this international celebrity was calmly standing in line for two hamburgers for a hungry little girl.

He came back swinging a bag and remarked, "I'm amazed that hamburgers are so cheap." (It must have been a long time since he bought any.}

At last, we walked into our living room where John had a cheerful fire blazing. He told Bill to take off his coat. Bill complied with alacrity and proceeded to slouch on the sofa, the same familiar posture seen on *Firing Line*. It was as if he had stepped out of the screen and onto my sofa.

Conversation flowed smoothly while Bill sipped a dry Martini. "That's a lot of propaganda," he remarked, pointing to the stack of his latest books and a copy of *National Review*, which I had strategically put on the coffee table.

"Yes," I replied sheepishly. "I can answer your book title *Did You Ever See a Dream Walking?* I surely did when William F. Buckley, Jr. walked into my living room."

He grinned engagingly. His blue eyes twinkled with intelligence. But, perhaps what attracted me most was his face: so open and honest. It was deeply suntanned and his nose was beet red.

John and Bill hit it off immediately. A great hunting buff, John launched forth into his latest quail hunting expedition. "I used to hunt quail on horseback in South Carolina, where my mother lived," Bill said.

I had read about Kamschatka, the Louisiana riverboat style house in Camden, South Carolina. An architect was asked to redesign the staircase 14 times. John was very glad he wasn't that architect.

Everyone was at ease. Bill has the gift of making strangers feel like old friends. He is one of the warmest, most gracious, genuinely charming people we've ever met. We had wondered if he would be the supercilious snob that he sometimes appears to be on television.

I asked John to take some pictures, and he clicked off shot after shot while jumping around like an experienced free-lance photographer getting scoops. I was elated, thinking how Gus and I would cherish the pictures and of how we would show our friends the intimate shots of us with the great William F. Buckley, Jr. Unfortunately, a week later John called me at my office and said, "Listen, honey, the pictures didn't turn out well."

"What happened?" I demanded.

"I f-f-forgot to plug in the right flash attachment," he sputtered. "Invite him again," he suggested lamely.

But, our evening with Bill as our guest was a success in all other ways. We had a French dinner: fresh artichokes with a vinaigrette sauce, fresh smoked trout that John had caught on his latest fishing trip, and tomatoes farcis with fresh sautéed mushrooms. We had three different wines, starting with a Pouilli Fuisée, Gus' and Mariette's contribution, followed by a dry Alsace, and we finished with a Pommard, along with French cheeses and fresh fruits. When we served a liqueur made of prunes, Buckley exclaimed, "Ah, slivovitza! I had some on my recent trip to Romania."

"I picked it up when I was over there two years ago," I explained.

While he smoked one of John's cigars, Marcelle, age ten at the time, walked in, looked at him disapprovingly and primly said, "Smoking is bad for you."

"Smoking is like a flattery, Marcelle," Buckley replied smoothly. "Neither one hurts if you do not inhale."

I had read that several Buckleys are chain smokers and that their father had strongly discouraged his brood's addiction to nicotine.

While Bill puffed and puffed his cigar, he remarked that one can't get Cuban cigars now. "I have to content myself with Dutch cigars, which are really quite good."

During our discussion on the situation in Cuba today, I was reminded of an experience I had in Romania with a Cuban Communist delegation staying at my hotel. One night I joined their table conversation. "Tell me the truth," I said to a member, who had obviously lived in Cuba before and after Castro, "how are things in Cuba now?"

The man looked furtively to the right, to the left, under the table, behind him and above his head. Pulling his chair closer to mine, he whispered, "Terrible!"

Bill threw back his head, laughed, and responded with one of his favorite stories about a visitor to Spain asking a college student if he liked Franco. The boy replied, "Follow me."

They got into a car, drove to remote woods outside Madrid and stopped, got out and walked a few paces. The student moved closer to his inquisitor and whispered, "Yes."

After dinner, Bill played several classical selections on the piano. Bach is a favorite of his. Soon, he called for a guitar and started strumming Spanish tunes, hugging the guitar and dancing with it. We, then, sang several duets in Spanish and French, which the others insisted they enjoyed.

I wasn't at all surprised at Bill's versatility. I had read that all the Buckleys were tutored in such diverse subjects as banjo, bird watching, calligraphy, carpentry, canoeing, driving, trotting horses, and folk dancing.

I asked Bill, "From the guests you have interviewed on *Firing Line*, which was the most colorful?"

He unequivocally replied, "Governor George Wallace. He was not only colorful, but the rudest and crudest guest I ever had on the program."

With the most memorable 'guest' in our house, the evening ended late, and Bill and I have remained friends ever since.

Globe Trotting

No longer being involved in the Atlanta Chamber on a daily basis meant I lost out on a great many free travel opportunities. After John and I remarried, he told me that he would never tell me I couldn't go somewhere; however, I would need to find a means of financing my own travels. This I did. I joined a travel agency as a sales representative. People in the travel industry get invited on all sorts of familiarization trips in order to acquaint them with the airlines that serve a specific destination, the hotels at the destination, and the sightseeing opportunities.

At the time, I had a live-in housekeeper, and my mother was always there to help. As I look back on all these trips I took without John, a momentary sense of guilt comes over me. But, it doesn't last long because he abhorred the social life and had little interest in anything that took him away from his work and his farm. He was happy not to go. On the other hand, I looked forward to every travel opportunity.

I earned my way, while booking travel accommodations for business travel, family vacations, and special cruises, in order to be eligible for the free trips that come with the territory.

After returning from a number of my trips, I've written articles about my experiences. Here are a few of the many articles that I wrote after returning home to Atlanta.

the odyssey of the little GOLD BOTTLE

Editor's Note: Mrs. Cunningham, an Atlanta housewife who speaks five foreign languages, frequently entertains foreign visitors to Georgia. Strictly on her own initiative she often presents them miniature gold key chains advertising Coca-Cola furnished her by George Montgomery, executive vice president of The Atlanta Coca-Cola Bottling Company. When she toured Europe recently Mrs. Cunningham carried a supply of key chains to give away as tokens of international friendship and goodwill. In the following article she describes the friendly and surprising reactions to her people-to-people mission.

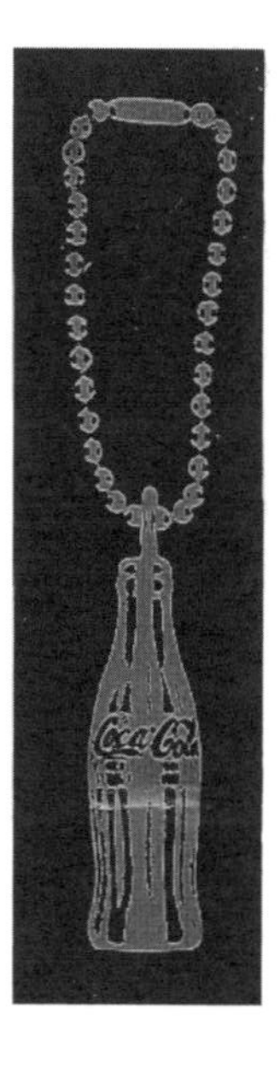

The Odyssey of the Little Gold Bottle

If you ever go to Venice, ask or look for Aldo's gondola. It carries a miniature golden Coca-Cola bottle on a key chain as a good luck charm.

I never dreamed that the dozen or so key chains I dropped into my suitcase before departing for Europe would create such a "chain" of reactions and unforgettable experiences. I called them "the golden talismans."

At first, to Aldo, I was just another tourist. But, as he rowed me skillfully through the canals around the liquid streets and I spoke to him about his city in Italian, he gradually lost his reserve, and we became friends. He told me that only Venetians and sons of gondoliers could become full-fledged gondoliers. A gondolier must work ten years under an older gondolier before he can work with his own union card. Only after ten years is he entitled to own his own gondola.

A gay-looking motorboat; bearing cases of Coca-Cola, passed by. I explained that I was from Atlanta, which is the home of Coca-Cola. Remembering the little golden bottles I had in my handbag, I gave him one. He was delighted and flattered that I should give him something. He immediately hung it on his gondola. The Venetian gondoliers are very superstitious and carry all sorts of good luck charms.

It even happened in Paris. I was on my way to Alexandre's, the famous hairdresser's, to have my hair styled. And due to a traffic jam created by DeGaulle's arrival from the airport with the King of Morocco, my taxi, along with hundreds of other vehicles, was stranded.

Since the cab could not move anyway, I hopped out and headed for an elegant candy store. Perhaps, it would be better to munch candy, rather than keep biting my fingernails. The owner waited on me. As the traffic outside was still not moving, I described my plight with the usual Gaelic effervescence: "I was on my way to Alexandre's, etc., on my last day in Paris, etc., and I was going to miss the precious coveted appointment so difficult to get, etc., etc."

In about two minutes we were fast friends, and he was telling me about his little boy of seven. On an impulse, I handed him the little golden miniature bottle for his boy, explaining at the same time that I was from Atlanta and that Atlanta was the home of Coca-Cola. He looked appreciatively at the small object and overwhelmed by my gesture, gave me some imported almond candy with the wish that it might make the contemplated wait at the hairdresser's more endurable. The traffic began to move. With a quick "au revoir," I hopped back into the taxi.

An hour later I was sitting in a room of the tremendous beauty salon. There was such vitality in the air and so much going on that I felt that something exciting was happening and something wonderful was bound to happen to me. I listened with awe at some of the famous names being paged, the Countess "X", the Baroness "M." Then I heard my own.

Rose in Paris wearing *Alexandre's* Coiffeur

Who could want me at Alexandre's I wondered, astonished! I looked up and there was the little man from the candy store. On his face there was a big smile, in his hands a large box of expensive chocolates. "This is for you, Madame. It is my son who sends it." He kissed my hand and with a most satisfied look on his face, departed.

Similar situations happened all over Europe. I was amazed that this little Coke bottle, when given under the right circumstances, would create such goodwill.

While dining in Rome at Alfredo's, I was startled by the sound of trumpets and only slightly recovered when Alfredo, owner and chef, with his entourage of waiters marched over to my table with a platter of fettuccini in one hand and in the other the golden fork and spoon given to him by Douglas Fairbanks and Mary Pickford. He had chosen my table to honor with his "king of fettuccini touch." With swiftness and tremendous vitality, like a maestro conducting Tchaikovsky's Concerto No. 1, he proceeded to mix the cheese with the noodles. As a crowning honor, Alfredo let me use the traditional gold spoon and fork. The gold of the spoon reminded me of the gold on the bottle, so I immediately took one out and gave it to Alfredo.

"Ah, Coca-Cola!" he exclaimed. I know that Atlanta in Georgia is the home of Coca-Cola." When he heard that Atlanta was also my home, his eyes sparkled, and his joy was contagious. He brought to the table a bottle of champagne along with his four musicians, and we all sipped champagne to the tune of "I'm a Rambling Wreck from Georgia Tech." Then, he brought over a huge scrapbook with all sorts of articles and pictures about him during his tour of the U.S.A. Alfredo was telling me with great spirit about his visit to Atlanta. We parted like old friends.

One afternoon in Rome, I wanted to visit the old Roman Forum. I boarded a local bus. After a lot of discussion, hand gesticulating and head shaking, I found I was on the right bus but going in the opposite direction. The conductor, young and friendly, explained to me that we were approaching the end of the line and I could ride back on the same bus, since it passed by the Forum on the way back to town. It was the sensible thing to do. The last passenger got off and the conductor and I struck up a lively conversation. It is the only way one can converse in Italy. We kept laughing because when I couldn't always find the right word or even the right sentence, I would bring out a tiny red dictionary that I always carried with me. He asked me where I lived, and I told him. He had never heard of Atlanta. I explained about the South, the country of *Gone with the Wind* and Coca-Cola. That prompted signs of recognition. "*Ah! Coca-Cola ¡ Si! mi piace! I like it*!" Then, I remembered and brought out a key chain. At first he looked at it with surprise and asked, "Oro? Gold?" When I shook my head and told him to keep it, his face glowed with appreciation. He immediately took out his old key chain and changed all the keys to the new one.

I will always remember the grateful smile of the beautiful French stewardess on board the sightseeing boat gliding on the Seine. How can I forget the star-filled eyes of the little boy in the subway, the appreciative thanks of the horse-and-buggy driver in Ischia? They are old friends now.

And while my children are admiring the two beautiful handmade leather napkin rings from Florence, two delighted Florentine children are probably playing with the tiny golden Coca-Cola bottles symbolizing the friendship that people around the world associate with Coke.

Before we abandon the subject of travel, I did put my travels to good use as the source of material for numerous travel articles for magazines that appeal to general readers and to people within the travel industry. The articles described my experiences at the destinations I visited. Here is one short example written for travel agency representatives.

Como and Its Lakes

Como is accessible from Rome by train, or you can arrange for a flight into Milan and then a rental car. The driving distance is only 30 minutes north across the Lombardy Plain. Como is a lively city. The silk capital of Europe, it is located at the extreme end of Lake Como.

A must is a visit to the Duomo, an imposing marble structure from the 15th century, with lavish decorations on its façade by the Rodari brothers. The hanging tapestries inside are world famous.

You might suggest an early stroll through the narrow streets in the shopping district, barred to automobiles and offering a multitude of exciting boutiques, followed by a visit to the port and the purchase of a ticket to tour the lake.

For those in a hurry, the *aliscafi* (hydrofoil) offers a quick transport across to Bellagio and Lecco. Or clients can take the slower *vaporetto* which stops at every village around the lake with such exotic names as Domeso, Tremezzo, Cernobbio, Cadennabia, Varenna, Menaggio, and Torno. These ports of call lure the visitor for a different kind of experience, the kind that inspired poets such as Goethe, Shelley, and Longfellow, as well as composers such as Verdi and Wagner.

Suggest a stop at Torno, a small forgotten world that belongs to the time of wandering minstrels, or isolated villages, complete with an old church, Santa Tecla, whose bells ring every hour on the hour.

The winding cobblestone streets lead to Villa Flora on the hill, famous for its cuisine. Here, the proud owner, Salvatore, will cook a superb fettuccini at the table. While dining al fresco on the tiled terrace, only the view will surpass Salvatore's culinary talents. Combine the green hills and snow-capped mountains, a dash of ski, a generous measure of shimmering water tinted blue-green, a myriad of distant red roofed villas, a profusion of rich vegetation with all sorts of wild flowers and … presto! Another gourmet feast.

For jet-setter accommodations, you might choose the luxurious *Villa D'Este* at Cernobbio. The Villa was started for Cardinal Gallio in 1589 and turned into a deluxe hotel in 1875. Today, it boasts a large dining room, a swimming pool, and an 18-hole golf course open year-round. The cardinal would have envied it. Or, you might book the *Grand Hotel Villa Serbelloni* in Bellagio. The town itself is at the point of Como's inverted "y" and the Villa, now owned by the Rockefeller Foundation, crowns a hill offering superb view of all three arms of the lake.

Bellagio, "The Pearl of the Larius," has intricate alleys and squares with flights of terraced steps that intersect at different levels. Here clients can purchase a work of art by a local artist of indulge in a savory pizza at the sidewalk café.

The *vaporetto* also stops at Moltrasio, famous for the visits of composer Bellini, who composed "Norma" and "Somnanbulla."

Farther down the lake stands Tremezzo, proud of its jewel, the Villa Carlota with its spectacular park filled with blooming azaleas, marble statues, and cascades.

The entire shore at Tremezzo is a succession of magnificent villas, hotels, and gardens.

In Varenna, near the central fork of the lake, one can have a fine lunch at the *Hotel-du-Lac*, then stroll through the ornate grounds of the Villa Monastero nearby and photograph the famed rose garden.

Before their return to Como, clients should stop at Brunate, where a funicular will take them 3,000 feet above the lake.

"The Terrace of the Alps" offers an unforgettable view over the lower basin of the lake and the Alps. There is a restaurant at the tip where visitors can sip an aromatic cappuccino and enjoy the incomparable view of the lake. Then night falls, lights turn on along the shore and, as the last ferry pulls away from the dock, they will wish they could stay forever.

1988

Bobby McFerrin advises everyone "Don't Worry, Be Happy"- but Americans do worry when Yellowstone National Park burns rampantly for months on end, and when Surgeon General C. Everett Koop reports that nicotine is addictive as heroine and cocaine. Televangelist Jimmy Swaggart confesses to soliciting sex from prostitutes. Oliver North and John Poindexter are accused of conspiracy to defraud the US government. The Soviets leave Afghanistan and the Iran-Iraq War comes to an end, but fears escalate when Libyan terrorists plant a bomb on Pan Am flight 103 that kills 270 people. George "Read My Lips" Bush becomes president of the United States, CDs outsell vinyl for the first time, and work is begun on the Chunnel. Seoul, Korea hosts the Summer Olympics and the Winter Games are in Calgary, Canada. A delegation (including Rose Cunningham) is sent before the International Olympic Committee to begin the lobbying process in order for the Olympics to come to the States... and Atlanta, GA.

My Olympic Experience

In late August 1988, I received a phone call from Horace Sibley, a prominent Atlanta attorney whom I knew from my Chamber days. Horace asked me to meet him at the Ritz Carlton for lunch. Over our meal we chatted about various things, including my work as honorary consul for Costa Rica and my recent trip there. Horace eventually got around to his reason for our meeting. "Rose," he said, "you know we're bidding for the 1996 Olympics, and I'm curious about your languages. How many do you speak fluently?"

I told him five, and he continued, saying that Billy Payne had asked him if he thought I might be interested in becoming an interpreter for the Atlanta Organizing Committee for the Olympic Games? If I was, they wanted me to go with them to Seoul, Korea for the 1988 Summer Olympics as an official representative of the city. Before I could respond, he quickly added, "We can cover all your travel expenses: however, we aren't in a position to offer a salary."

I told Horace that I would have to talk it over with my husband and let him know later that evening. Of course, on the way home I knew very well that I was going to go.

A few weeks later, on September 13th, I left on a flight headed for Seoul, via Portland. As it turned out, I was the only interpreter who traveled with the Atlanta Organizing Committee. Among those on board were: Billy Payne, the president of the Atlanta Committee; Mayor Andrew Young, who was honorary chairman of our group; public relations expert Bob Kohn; sports editor Furman Bischer; Albert "Smitty" Smith the charming chef from the Ritz Carlton who was in charge of our entertaining; various representatives of Atlanta's leading corporations; and certain wealthy individuals who were part of the Atlanta power structure. Throughout our trip to Seoul, I enjoyed the company of all of them. Our group flew from Atlanta to Portland, then transferred to another plane for a grueling 17-hour flight to Seoul.

At 5:20 P.M. the next day, we landed at Kempo Airport. Before leaving the plane, all passengers were asked not to take any pictures in or around the airport. I assume this was linked with Seoul's security procedures.

Our Atlanta group was supposed to be met at the airport by the Coca-Cola van, but it didn't appear. We piled into cabs with our luggage and headed for our hotel. Already, I had the opportunity to use my limited number of Korean words and phrases and was determined to expand my knowledge of the language while there.

As we moved through the streets, my first impressions were that the city seemed quite spread out. Most buildings had colorful tile roofs that were curved at the bottom in the Oriental fashion. The massive amount of traffic, while very slow, was conducted in an orderly way, the people were very well dressed, and the city was bubbling with activity. There were huge, colorful banners everywhere, waving their message of welcome in multiple languages. Seoul's hosting of the Olympics was putting Atlanta's hosting of the Democratic Convention earlier that year to shame. We learned that Seoul was spending a million dollars a day on the Olympics. Every penny of it showed.

By the time we arrived at the Shilla Hotel, we had run up a taxi fare of 4600 wons (roughly $6.60). It was clear that our American concept of costs was not going to be applicable here. The Shilla, Seoul's finest and headquarters for the event, was elegant and beautiful. It was sited atop a hill and surrounded by a lovely garden, set apart from hustle and bustle of the city below. The windows of my room allowed me an amazing view of the Seoul Tower, a busy highway, and two stadiums.

Even though I treated myself to a 9000 wons massage ($13), my body kept telling me to wake up because it was seven in the morning in Atlanta. I realized adjusting to the time difference was going to take awhile.

The next morning, Horace met me in the lobby for coffee, and we happened to meet a few of the IOC, International Olympic Committee, representatives who were also staying at the Shilla. These members, I later learned, had to be treated like royalty or heads of state. They were the ones who had the power to vote for a city ... or against it. Everywhere there were banners, signs, and balloons. As Horace and I moved through the hotel lobby, we could hear what seemed like hundreds of languages being spoken. It was a truly international event, and I loved the excitement of it all.

After coffee, a meeting of the Atlanta Committee was held in Horace's room. That was the first time I met Billy Payne, the driving force of our group and the man who started Atlanta's Olympic movement. He was a tall, personable man. One look at this attorney and you automatically knew he had been a college football star in his teens.

Charlie Battle, our PR pro, went over our strategies, which included lunches, dinners, and small receptions at a house the Committee had rented. We had with us the chef from the Ritz Carlton, and his job was to impress our guests with the quality of food Atlanta had waiting for visitors to our city. I was assigned the task of writing invitations and serving as Billy Payne's translator when he addressed the IOC members.

In fact, I was the only translator among us. Other than Andrew Young, I was also the only one who brought an international presence to our group.

Still, Horace was opposed to my playing up my Costa Rican connection. I viewed his decision as a huge mistake because my connections added an extra dimension that he could capitalize on, especially with the Latin IOC members. Horace had a strictly Atlanta mentality and was slow to realize that the IOC members were accustomed to other countries using their diplomatic corps to lure the Olympics to their sites.

The competition for the 1999 winter Olympic site was between Alaska, Sweden, Bulgaria, and Norway. That evening Norway was announced the winner, and its delegation hosted a huge reception to celebrate their being chosen.

At this celebration, the organizing director for Albertville told me it was the charm of the people that really sells a city. "But, you must cultivate each of the members of the International Olympic Committee," he cautioned.

While the total number of members occasionally changes, there were 92 at that time. We did our best to get to know each one personally. I made some personal friends among them, and one of my favorites was Augustin Arroyo and his charming wife Raquel from Ecuador. Later, it was sad hearing that he was fired from the Olympic Committee for fraud.

The city was filling up with dignitaries, the famous, and - most notably - Europe's royalty. Among those I recall were The King of Sweden, Queen Sophia of Spain, Prince Albert of Monaco, and Princess Nora of Liechtenstein who was conducting an educational project in Costa Rica. If a royal was in your hotel (Princess Ann and Queen Sophia were among those at Shilla), it was not unusual to spot them in the elevator, wearing a bathrobe en route to or from the pool or sauna.

It was during this adventure that I was introduced to the jet set and how the rich and powerful operate. I had thought, from my work through the Chamber, that I knew, but I had only experienced a glimpse of what they expect and what they receive. They enjoy lives of luxury, limousines and private jets, pampering and parties. Gifts seem to rain down on them, and their power is simply enormous.

Most IOC members are chosen because they are extremely wealthy, are royalty, very influential in their country, and/or were gold medal winners who parlayed those medals into wealth and prestige. Furthermore, a new member has to have inside ties - friends who want to have him or her voted into their exclusive ranks. Since membership means voting power, all members are heavily courted by the competing cities.

Some were charming; some were definitely not. For example, the IOC member from Cuba was obnoxious, arrogant, and aloof. In fact, all the representatives from Communist countries were very distant and worked quite hard at not being friendly. In Seoul, for example, when the Romanian IOC committee member learned that I spoke his language, he clammed up and wouldn't speak to me, avoiding me anytime we were in proximity of one another. I think he was afraid. He didn't know who I was and was afraid I might have been planted there by the Communist Party to check on him. Suspicion and paranoia are very much a part of life in a police state. It was something I could understand on an intellectual level, having lived on the run for much of my youth, but it was still a disappointment. I really wanted to talk to him about my native country and could have been a great help to him as an interpreter.

By the time the 1996 Olympics took place, Romania's Communist government had been overthrown, and he was no longer a member of the Communist Party. He had, by then, moved up in the new government and greeted me like a long-lost friend. His was not an unusual case. Many former Communists managed the fancy footwork necessary to not only survive the transition from Communism, but also to move on to greater authority. It was, for them, little more than a change of hats.

The traffic from our hotel to the opening ceremonies was horrendous. But, we had no right to complain because from hotels further removed, the trip took hours. Seoul is a city of ten million, very spread out, and many of the taxi drivers didn't even know where the major hotels were. If you wanted to get anywhere, you needed to take a card with you that included directions. Otherwise, you would be lost.

The opening ceremonies, we were told, cost the equivalent of nine million dollars. Once again, every penny showed. The pageantry and the spectacle, teamed with the introduction of 12,000 athletes from 160 countries, were breathtaking. Everything supported the theme *One World*. In his opening remarks, Seoul's chief organizer said, "Our world has overcome many obstacles, but here we are together."

It was a highly appropriate theme and statement because this was the first time in twelve years that all the major countries were represented at the Olympics. It had been President Jimmy Carter's decision that the United States did not attend the Moscow Olympics, and four years later Russia retaliated by boycotting the games in Los Angeles. The Koreans had every right to be proud of their committee's accomplishments.

There were 70,000 spectators for the opening ceremonies. Under each person's seat was a plastic bag that contained a raincoat, a whistle, a sun visor, a colored card to hold up on command, and earphones that translated the opening ceremonies in the language of your choice. As I recall, there must have been nine or ten from which you could choose.

The two-and-a-half hour opening ceremony included more than 2,000 performers. Korean dancers in brilliantly colored costumes, a sky filled with red, white, and blue balloons, more dancers symbolizing the Vestal Virgins of the Greek era, the Asian Taek Wan Do wrestlers and on and on. The 76 parachutists landing in the stadium was my favorite portion of the entertainment. They used their colored parachutes to form the Olympic rings.

The spectacle was simply overwhelming; yet, it did not surpass the thrill of seeing the athletes' entrance. The procession is always lead by Greece, in honor of its creation of the original Olympics. The honor of entering second always goes to the host country, and the remaining 158 countries were arranged in alphabetical order following Seoul's teams. Each group wore colors or costumes that represented their nation. The half-naked Mongolians were standouts in this respect.

For each team there was a national theme or song. For example, Canada entered to the tune of "Alouette," while throwing Frisbees to the crowd. I personally found the U.S. team of 700 an embarrassment. They entered in an orderly fashion, like the rest: however, as they circled the stadium, they abandoned their lines and behaved like spoiled children, taking photographs of each other and holding up huge signs for NBC's cameras with personal messages to family, lovers, and friends. I thought it showed a complete disrespect for the event and the other countries involved.

I was particularly proud of the 15-member Costa Rican team. It was lead by swimmer Sylvia Poll, carrying their nation's flag. Later in Atlanta, her sister Claudia would win a gold medal in swimming competition. It was not only Costa Rica's first gold medal, it was also the first won by a representative of any Central American country.

The finale was a release of doves that was teamed with more dancers, small children, and huge balloons, depicting the mascot of the Seoul Olympics - the Hundori tiger.

We made a point of collecting as much cost information on the event as possible. Seoul had been announced the 1988 host six years prior to the event. Immediately following the announcement, their committee began an intensive international campaign to build their facilities, spending one billion dollars on the construction of their stadiums. After the Olympics, the stadiums' presence would assure Seoul of being the sports capital of Asia.

It was hoped that the IOC's choice of South Korea would lead to the unification of South and North Korea; however, at the time I am writing, that still seems a distant dream. In fact, North Korea decided not to participate in these Olympic Games.

I found the awarding of the medals after each event very impressive and filled with national pride as the flag of each first, second, and third place winner's country was raised and their national anthem played.

Along with our politicking and information gathering, we did manage to see some of the competitions. I was fortunate to witness the 100-meter women's swimming event in which U.S. team member Jane Evans broke her own world record. It was thrilling hearing our national anthem played and watching our flag being raised.

When I spotted the Costa Rican group seated across the stadium, I went to join them when Sylvia Poll won her Silver Medal in swimming. The little group was easy to spot because Costa Rica's ambassador to South Korea was holding their flag high.

The next day there was a meeting where Billy Payne required my translation skills. The occasion was a luncheon hosted by the former Korean ambassador to Costa Rica, Mr. Parks. He and I had originally met in Atlanta when Gonzalo Facio was Foreign Minister of Costa Rica. At the luncheon, I translated Payne's remarks into French because our host spoke French, but not English. Along with the dignitaries present, there were a number of Costa Rican athletes.

It was at this luncheon that Arroyo Augustine told me about having been at the Berlin Olympics in 1936. He said that the president of the IOC Committee told Hitler that he could not make a speech and could only say "I declare the Games officially opened." This long-standing rule could not be violated.

Hitler replied, "You are telling me that after all the money we've spent, in my own country, I cannot make a speech? I inform you that I will."

The president of the IOC, an American, quickly responded, "Make your speech if you like, but as soon as you have finished, I will announce that Rule Number Ten has been violated, and I will declare the Olympic Games canceled."

We know from the extensive film coverage of the Berlin Games that Hitler only said the permissible sentence.

I mention his telling of this story because it illustrates one of the qualities of the International Olympic Committee that I greatly admire. Despite their flaws and arrogance, they have rules, and have the power to enforce them. At the same time, I know that the rules have been bent from time to time, but the Committee does have the power and position to demand respect for its standards.

The situations that cause rules to be bent all seem to deal with money. With each succeeding Olympics, the dollar amounts invested grow and grow, turning what was once a friendly competition into a financial feeding frenzy for television and for some Olympic Committee members who have abused the system. This is a subject that I will cover in more detail later.

While there was much to see and do, scores of people to meet and establish friendly relations with, I also had my writing and interpreting duties, which had to come first. The most important function I served was as Billy Payne's interpreter during his audience with Antonio Samaranch, who served as President of the Olympic Committee for many years. Samaranch was the shogun of the Olympics, omnipotent and feared. Interestingly, it wasn't his size that intimidated, for he was quite small and looked even more so next to a man of Payne's physical stature.

From the beginning, I had no reason to like Samaranch because he had been a Nazi sympathizer. In my view, he was arrogant, unfriendly, and a master at condescension. For example, even though he spoke flawless English, he insisted on Payne's interview being held in French, the official language of the Olympics. Why? To demean Billy Payne and place him at a distinct disadvantage because Payne was an American. That's my opinion.

Back and forth, back and forth, I translated each man's remarks, while Samaranch understood everything, even without my translating for him. Eventually, however, Samaranch did lapse into English. That was not until shortly before the conclusion of the meeting, and, Samaranch never made eye contact with anyone.

I considered most of the Committee members spoiled prima donnas who were outrageously catered to by the bidding cities. When Andy Young saw how the game was played, he jokingly said, "When I die, I want to come back as an IOC member." It was most educational to me, a newcomer to the Olympic world, to witness the competition for the right to become an Olympic site.

It takes years of cultivation of each member of this Committee, in addition to the millions required to build stadiums, Olympic Villages, and other facilities to their liking. The cities are expected to court the members with invitations to visit the prospective sites. These invitations had to include the Committee member's spouse, involve first-class transportation, deluxe accommodations, the finest food, and gifts not to exceed a value of 35 dollars.

However, I've seen gifts of much greater value. Also, plane tickets had to be redeemable for cash. That meant Committee members could often pocket a considerable amount of change. For example, a member of the Committee visiting Atlanta could schedule a trip to Canada to visit a potential winter Olympics site the following week. He could then cash in the plane tickets and take a less expensive flight from Atlanta to Canada and do as he pleased with the extra money.

Keep in mind that these tickets could easily represent a cost of ten thousand dollars per trip. And, despite the fact that using travel to possible sites in order to line one's pockets was strictly against Olympic rules, in actuality there were no limits on the number of trips a member might request. There might be two or more visits "required" to help an undecided person make up his or her mind during the six years of this courtship. It is extremely important to cultivate the members on a continuous basis. You pay the price.

During my translation experiences, especially those involving certain African nations, Committee members not only asked but expected to be invited; they had their diplomatic code for letting you know exactly what perks they anticipated. For example, one IOC member told us he had heard such wonderful things about certain medical facilities in Atlanta and just happened to mention the medical treatments that most interested him. That translated into open-heart surgery for him and eye surgery for his wife. Another country's representative delivered his coded demand for scholarships, uniforms, aid, and other requirements. Toronto, Manchester, Athens, and Atlanta were the four competing cities that were expected to woo the 92 members of the Committee.

My job was to translate whenever a member of the International Olympic Committee met with Atlantans and could not express himself in English. I translated the member's remarks, usually to Mayor Andrew Young, and then translated Andy's reply.

I found it interesting how much the advice given us by the various Committee members conflicted. One IOC member told me to get the word out among our group not to pursue our quest for the 1996 Games. "You will spend a great deal of money and stand no chance at all with the Committee because Athens is the favorite. Besides, no city is ever selected the first time they try. Besides, you don't have all the necessary facilities."

Still, I knew that Atlanta had the ability to build anything we lacked and was long on charm. In fact, Billy Payne had the brilliant idea of having files set up on each Olympic Committee member. In addition to good wishes on their special day, we sent a small gift, such as a book, about our city.

A few were more personal choices. For example, when we learned the IOC member from Cuba wanted a bull terrier, we sent him one. We know from the feedback that these remembrances were well received and made an enormous impression without having involved much capital outlay. Clearly charm and personal attention and building whatever might be needed were second nature to our bidding committee. The problem in my mind was could we handle the logistics, the day-to-day operation of an event of this magnitude?

Still, the major message that we received from all the IOC was, "What can you do for us? – even though we might or might not choose your city." The African countries, however, all told us quite clearly that they would vote for Atlanta because of their high regard for Andrew Young. Still, I wondered at what price?

We also had the Arab countries' votes. At that time, Arab royalty was making sizeable investments in Georgia real estate, which may have been a factor. I was particularly impressed with Mohammed Mazali, former Foreign Minister of Tunisia, who made an unusual request. He lived in exile in Paris after escaping from Tunisia when Bourguiba came to power. Mazali asked the mayor's help in talking to senators on his behalf. He wanted to come to the United States to discuss his political position with members of Congress and get his message delivered to the President of the United States. Andrew Young said he would see what he could do but would only be able to help him if the Democrats won. Unfortunately for Mazali, Republican Ronald Reagan won the election.

While in Seoul, I caught the Olympic pin trading fever. Some called it lunacy. As we went up and down elevators, I found myself admiring the collections various people had pinned onto their coats and hats. Conversation would lead to trading, and soon I had a considerable collection. The more countries' pins you acquired, the more respect you were shown. As a representative of Atlanta, the sight of my pin collection labeled me as having contacts in scores of countries. I collected these for my grandchildren, and at the 1996 Olympics each proudly wore a vest covered in the pins I had collected by trading Atlanta bidding pins and later trading Atlanta Olympic pins.

In addition to my translating and speech writing, there was time to enjoy the events and get to know the city of Seoul. A phenomenon there was a section of town known as Ittawa, a three-mile long strip of shops, bars, and discos that were just minutes from the Shilla Hotel. Ittawa translates *street of bargains*, and that was exactly what it was. Clothing was the best buy. Tailor shops would measure you, let you choose your material and style. Within 48 hours you had a fabulous new suit. The price for a man or woman's suit ranged from eighty to a hundred and fifty dollars.

One man in our delegation bought five suits of the finest material. Readymade silk dresses were fifty dollars, in contrast with Atlanta prices of more than three hundred dollars for similar quality. It was also the home of knock-offs, exact imitations of couture fashion accessories, such as scarves and bags, all available for pennies on the dollar. I saw a copy of a Hermes scarf that sold for three hundred fifty dollars in Paris; in Seoul, the price was ten dollars. Another example: for twenty dollars you could have an exact copy of 850-dollar leather Chanel bag. Watches, jade, topaz, amethyst, and other jewelry were everywhere you looked in Ittawa. It was here that most visitors collected the souvenirs that they took home with their pin collections. The Olympics definitely resulted in a tremendous boost in the South Korean economy.

After returning to Atlanta, Billy Payne sent me to visit the Committee members from Peru and Uruguay both of whom I had befriended while in Seoul. My trip to Uruguay had an ominous beginning: canceled flights and much confusion. A little later than planned, I finally arrived in Montevideo, Uruguay's capital, which is proud of its 97 percent literacy rate, a statistic that certainly sets it apart from most of South America.

The IOC member in Uruguay was José Vallarino; a man in his mid seventies who liked his Johnny Walker on the rocks. And, he liked a lot of it. Vallarino was known by all as Pepe and was a talkative fellow who seemed eager to tell me about the internal politics of the IOC. He scheduled our first meeting in the bar of my hotel. After too long in the bar, I excused myself in order to catch up on my sleep, leaving him to have "just one more" for the road.

About ten o'clock the next morning, Pepe came for me in his beaten-up Volvo. It took only experiencing a few minutes of his driving, to understand why the car was in such deplorable condition. Poor vision, excessive drinking, and lack of driving skills are not a good combination. It was a miracle that he hadn't been in a serious accident, the way he took intersections so nonchalantly, which is a general Latin American habit.

Pepe told me that of all the candidate cities, Atlanta was the only one to come to see him, and he was genuinely touched by my visit. As we careened about the city, he confided that he believed Athens was incapable of guaranteeing a change in its poor economic situation and lack ed adequate security; that Toronto was well organized; while Belgrade, Manchester, and Melbourne were not viable contenders.

Even though it was still morning, he took me to the popular market for a cocktail: dry wine mixed with sweet wine, a concoction that any wine connoisseur would consider a sacrilege. The market was a popular dining place, dotted with numerous restaurants. As we continued our tour, Pepe pointed out historical monuments. Since he was a history professor and the author of two books (one on the French revolution and another on the Golden Age of Spain), he took great pleasure in relating the history of his country.

I quickly saw that he was a very popular fellow and deeply involved in the politics of his country. Everywhere we went people made an effort to speak to him. His Olympic ties went back to his youth when he was a champion Olympic rower. At the time of my visit, he was president of the Uruguayan Olympic Committee, a post he had held for thirty years, and he had been an IOC member since 1936. Despite his tenure, he was not on good terms with the Olympics' president, Samaranch.

Pepe had worn a variety of hats in his life. In addition to his Olympic connections, he was a retired bank manager, president of the local rowing club, and considered himself a farmer. He ran a small farm, which he named *La Chacra*, a modest name that simply means "the farm." *La Chacra* was his passion, and he insisted on showing it to me. This entailed a forty-mile drive north of the city, and I kept my eyes closed much of the way in order not to be scared witless by his driving.

On his farm, he had sheep, cattle, and one huge pig, his personal pet, which he kept chained to a post. This 75-hectare plot (roughly 181 acres) had a lovely orchard of lemons, oranges, and grapefruits ready to be picked. Also, it should be no surprise that he had a vineyard to make wine and that he insisted we sample a bit of it.

The farm's cottage was dirty and unkempt. The walls were lined with pictures of the King of Sweden, Castro, the Pope, and his wife, daughter, and granddaughter. All three of the ladies in his life had died of cancer. Since he attributed their deaths to eating red meat, he refused to touch it – even though his farm's principal product was livestock.

After the tour and wine sampling we headed back to the city, traveling through the countryside, which was parched by drought. When we returned, I invited Pepe to Atlanta. We then dined at a superb French restaurant as guests of the head of Coca-Cola operations in Uruguay.

Later, when Pepe Vallarino came to Atlanta for site inspection, John and I met him at the Marriott where other IOC members were staying. Billy Payne had asked us to entertain him because Pepe had clearly shown, as far back as the Seoul Olympic, that he enjoyed being with me. However, John and I did not give him the royal treatment that an IOC member usually receives. We picked him up at his hotel in John's red pickup truck and headed to our farm for the day. A bucket of Kentucky Fried Chicken, a bottle of wine, the cattle, and orchards translated into a grand time for Pepe.

During my visit to Uruguay, I learned that Jose Vallarino wanted a tractor for his farm, and I have little doubt that his hinting netted him five, one from each bidding city. When I moved on to Lima, Peru, I learned their need was for buses. The mayor of Lima, who happened to be the brother of Peru's IOC member, received a dozen. All it took was a call to the manufacturer.

By the time the Barcelona Olympics rolled around in 1992, the competition was over and no more diplomacy or courtship was going to alter the outcome. Those of us who were dispensable did not get to attend and add extra strain to the budget.

We were prepared not to be chosen as 1996 host city since it usually requires several qualifying steps to be selected. We also knew of the political maneuverings that can take place. For example: In the 1992 selections a compromise was reached. Paris would host the '92 Summer Games while Albertville would be the site of the '92 Winter Games. Those kinds of deals were made all the time; you give me Barcelona, I'll give you Albertville.

In our competition, Athens had a sentimental advantage. The 1996 Olympics would mark the hundredth anniversary of the modern Olympic Games and Athens, after all, was where the original Olympics began. Toronto had the advantage of having been the site of one of the most successful biddings in recent history, while Manchester was not, in my opinion, a serious contender. I think the whole world was surprised when, in 1990, at the IOC meeting, Samaranch made his announcement of the Committee's decision to award the 1996 Olympics to Atlanta.

Sadly, I had to watch that memorable event via television. I was supposed to go to Tokyo with Atlanta's organizing committee, but I came down with the flu and had to cancel my plans.

When the Atlanta committee returned from Tokyo in 1990, I was among those at the airport to greet them. However, I had no idea how different the set of rules would be following their return.

My connections with the committee took me in 1992 to the Barcelona Olympics as translator for the Czar of the 1996 Cultural Olympiad, Dr. Jeffrey Babcock, assuming I could find a place to stay. For a time, it seemed that wasn't going to happen because hotel rooms were scarce and expensive. However, something wonderful occurred I would have never anticipated – especially considering where it happened: the Grand Canyon.

In June, prior to the 1992 Olympics in Barcelona, John and I took the grandchildren to the Grand Canyon. While we were in the process of registering for our rooms, one of the front desk clerks was having a difficult time communicating with a couple who could not speak English. Hearing the frustrated couple speak Spanish, I offered to translate for them. In the process of speaking with the Spanish couple, I learned the man was a doctor from Barcelona and that they were on their honeymoon. The bride and groom were trying to get the clerk to understand that they very much wanted to go down the rapids and needed to know how to make arrangements.

I took care of it for them, and they were delighted. In exchange, they asked if there was anything they could do for me.

I stopped short of automatically saying, "No, but thank you for asking," and instead said, "Maybe there is. I'm planning a trip to Barcelona in July for the Olympics, but unless I find accommodations, I won't be able to go."

They quickly said there was no problem at all and offered the doctor's parents' apartment to me. "They aren't planning to stay in the city during the Olympics," they assured me, "The apartment is yours."

I quickly accepted their gracious offer, and one month later was on my way to Barcelona. Again, my knowledge of languages paid off.

The couple even met me at the airport and took me to the apartment, which was truly beautiful – not to mention free.

When one door closes, another often opens. Even though I my translating skills as a volunteer were no longer needed by the Atlanta Committee, that was not to be the end of my Olympic involvement. The Costa Rican Olympic Committee asked for my help in raising money for their athletes. With the challenge came another honorary title: Olympic Attaché of Costa Rica. Their athletes didn't even have the funds to pay for uniforms to wear during the events, and no lodging was prepared for them prior to check-in at the Olympic Village. I started contacting various companies that I knew had an interest in Costa Rica and asked them to help in any way they could. Through those requests, I raised the needed funds and found individuals who were glad to assist in other ways, such as with housing and meals.

A Costa Rican kayaker, Roger Madrigal, from Turrialba, stayed with John and me from the moment he arrived in Atlanta until it was time for him to move to the Olympic Village. I was even able to persuade Speedo to sponsor him. There was additional help for him, as well. George and Ginny Steffens, a couple from Memphis, Tennessee, who had once hired Roger as a white water rafting guide while visiting Costa Rica, also raised some money to help cover his expenses and provided a place for him to stay during the early training phase in the U.S.

I frequently took Valerie and her children, thirteen-year-old John and ten-year-old Ashley, with me to the Village, on a daily visit to Olympic Park to collect and swap pins. John's collection attracted the attention of network newscaster Tom Brokaw, who chatted with him on national television. John told Brokaw the thing he liked most about the entire Olympic experience was collecting pins.

If he had been asked what his second favorite thing was, it would surely have been receiving private coaching from the French skeet shooting team's coach. One afternoon, we took young John, who is an excellent shot, and the French coach to our farm, where we have a skeet range. There, the coach gave John pointers on how to improve his performance.

While many countries could afford to rent Atlanta's finest facilities for their exclusive use before and during the games and bring their own chefs and entertainment, such an extravagance was totally beyond Costa Rica's capabilities. So, I located individuals in Atlanta who welcomed the group and invited the team and its guests into their homes for dinner parties. I too entertained the group at our house.

Being an Olympic Attaché carries with it a carte blanche to attend any game and enjoy the best seats. It gave me access to the Olympic Village, private parties, and the right to share the experience with other guests. Valerie and her children accompanied me to dozens of events.

During preparation for the Games, as well as during the Olympics, I was continually in and out of the Olympic Village, taking care of some need or other for the Costa Rican athletes. For example, after their arrival in Atlanta, I was told they had no jackets to wear in the opening and closing ceremonies. I managed to raise the funds locally and find an Atlanta manufacturer who could produce jackets for them in time for the opening ceremony.

I've been asked, on several occasions, if there aren't individuals or companies in Costa Rica who could afford, at least, to meet the basic needs of these athletes? The answer is of course there are; however, few countries have a true sense of community, and none equals the United States in its belief and practice of sharing with and assisting others. Even the money raised in Costa Rica came primarily from U.S. companies operating there.

The experience I cherish most was marching in the Opening Ceremonies here in Atlanta. Marcelle, watching the Olympics in Paris, saw me on television, having the time of my life. There were only a dozen of us in the Costa Rican delegation, including the President of the Costa Rican Olympic Committee, the coaches, and the athletes.

It was an indescribable experience, walking into that stadium, which had been built for the Olympics (and later downsized and transformed into Turner Field), to look about and see 90,000 cheering people. I had goose pimples. While Atlanta's handling of vendors and traffic was not up to par and the 1996 Games' mascot "Izzy" was the laughing stock of the world, there was certainly no faulting the opening and closing ceremonies. Both set standards no one has surpassed.

The events the Costa Rican delegation competed in were boxing, kayaking, track, bicycling, and swimming. In swimming, Claudia Poll won the 200-meter free style gold medal, Costa Rica's first gold medal. Until this win, the silver medal her sister won in Seoul had been Costa Rica's single moment of glory in the whole Olympic competition. Just before Claudia went to the award ceremony, someone handed her a jacket to wear that had a prominent Pepsi-Cola logo. I saw it happen because I was nearby. I can't say whether or not, in all the excitement, anyone else noticed. Later, I was told that the person who gave her the jacket told the young swimmer that, if she wore it, she would receive a sizeable sum of money. Wearing it caused her to be disqualified. Later, however, Claudia was reinstated.

The IOC is very strict about athletes wearing sponsors' gear that is not part of their official uniform. So, while a basketball player may wear shoes provided by a sponsor who manufactures shoes or a swimmer may wear a bathing suit made by a company that sells swim wear, other items of apparel that feature product logos are not acceptable. I think they are correct in drawing this line; otherwise, athletes would be turned into walking billboards for their sponsors.

Sponsors are indispensable to the Olympic Games. For their massive infusion of money, they demand a lot and receive much of what they demand. First, they have to pay dearly to be recognized as an official sponsor, then they have to underwrite the financial needs of a contestant. Those costs can include transportation, housing, clothing, coaches, trainers, and on and on.

Atlanta, and, I assume, other host cities as well, had an office that strictly dealt with sponsors. Far more companies apply for the honor than receive it. It's a mix of finances and politics that determines who is and who isn't awarded the status. And there is value to the sponsor. Not only does sponsorship tie their name to the Olympics and reap the benefits of association, there is also the international exposure. For example, the Swiss manufacturer of an inexpensive sports watch, called Swatch, was virtually unknown before the Olympics. They gave away watches at the games, flooded television internationally with their advertising, resulting in the name of their product becoming a household word within a matter of weeks.

For many years, the majority of sponsors, however, have been U.S. companies. That circumstance often makes the U.S. unpopular in other countries.

Following the games in Salt Lake City, there was a great deal of press about corruption and extravagant gifts and other forms of bribery. A few IOC members were let go for such actions as pressing bidding cities into funneling money into an IOC member's private business in exchange for a vote. The major offenders were from Africa and South America. However, from what I was told, there were few who did not set prices on their votes.

In my opinion, Billy Payne is a hero, a hero who was mistreated by Atlanta's political structure. He brought us the Olympics and did a masterful job of controlling an international event that, by its nature, has countless opportunities to turn into disaster. It was a pleasure working with him and being a part of the dream he turned into a reality.

1990

The U.S.S.R. admits to the 1940 massacre of 15,000 Polish officers in Katyn, U.S. and the allies drive Iraq from Kuwait in the first war shown live on TV, Germany celebrates its formal reunification, and Akihito is proclaimed Japan's 125th Emperor. South Africa's President de Klerk lifts restrictions on 30 organization and grants amnesty for political prisoners, including Nelson Mandela while Rian Malan publishes *My Traitor's Heart* about life in South Africa. English and French engineers meet under the sea when the Channel sections are linked. In France the Dance Biennial becomes the largest-ever gathering of U.S. dance companies, while in the U.S. rap is the rage. And the music world loses Leonard Bernstein and Aaron Copland.

Teaching

In the summer of 1990, shortly after my mother's death, I felt a need to be more involved and active. Deciding that I needed a fresh opportunity to teach, I approached Mary Cobb, the head of Emory University's Evenings at Emory. Evenings at Emory are a nationally admired continuing education program that had been in operation for many years. I asked Mary about the possibility of an opening for a Spanish Instructor. While Evenings at Emory already had a Spanish teacher, John Stroud, Mary said that my timing was excellent because she was considering adding a class that would require an additional Spanish teacher. I applied for the position and was hired.

When Mary showed me the textbook that John was using, I said, "Mary, this is not what I want to teach. John is teaching grammar, and that's fine. However, it's not my approach to language."

I went on to explain that I believed that language should be taught the way a child learns a language: conversationally. In my opinion, grammatical structure comes later. The real motivation for learning a new language is to be able to communicate basic thoughts and needs.

Mary Cobb liked my concept and the idea of my writing my own conversational Spanish textbook. Much of the material, I already had in the form of handouts and worksheets that I had created for the classes I taught at the YMCA. But, Mary balked at the title I wanted to give the book. It translated *Where Is the Bathroom?* Our compromise became *¿Donde está?*, which means "Where is it?"

I structured the book to include the material covered in two eight-class series. It includes the words and phrases necessary to communicate on a variety of daily issues.

Even the other teacher decided I was on to something and switched to my textbook. John Stroud retired, but the Spanish Language Division of Evenings at Emory continued growing. It reached the point where I was teaching every weekday evening, which left me with no free time at night. So, Emory and I came to a mutually beneficial agreement. The Evenings at Emory program designated me as Coordinator of the Spanish Language Program, and I was to screen and subcontract with other qualified teachers.

Today my staff of four and I offer ten Spanish I classes and an additional six classes that cover Spanish 2, 3, and 4. Each session, I teach three of the twelve classes. For the remaining ones, I meet with each class its first time, then hand off to one of my staff. The system seems to work well, and the experience has certainly been an interesting one for me.

I begin each class by telling them that there are three things that cannot be translated: poetry, jokes, and insults. Each of the three is unique to a language.

It surprises many people that only a small number of those who sign up are adults wanting to brush up on their language skills in preparation for vacation travel abroad. Most of the students come in connection with their work. I've had television newscasters, such as Monica Kauffman, and CNN and Fox News personnel, take my classes in order to become more comfortable pronouncing Spanish names. Other students include scientists and other personnel from the Centers for Disease Control, contractors and business people who supervise crews of primarily Hispanic employees, business people who frequently have to conduct business deals with people from Latin America.

I even had an Atlanta Braves coach take my class in order to better communicate with the team's members whose native language is Spanish. I have a surprising number of students who want to improve their Spanish in order to communicate better with their in-laws. I had a traffic court judge from Loganville who, after two classes, came to me to say how much he enjoys the text book. But, he explains, the two words he desperately needs are not in it. "What are they?" I asked him.

"Guilty" and "Not Guilty." *"Culpable y no culpable."*

There are even Spanish majors with extensive grammatical training who still feel a need to improve their conversational skills; so, they sign up for "Rosita's class."

Another segment of my students is comprised of medical personnel who deal with patients who speak little English. For this group, I developed a special text. These classes started at Evenings at Emory for the School of Medicine and have included many of the hospitals in the Atlanta area.

In the winter of 1997, a friend called, saying that Westminster School, one of the leading private schools in Atlanta, was losing one of its Spanish teachers and was looking for a replacement, someone with significance in the teaching field. They felt I was the person for the job and asked if I was interested in at least filling in from March until the end of the school year? I saw this as an excellent opportunity to see how I would feel about a full-time position and accepted the offer to teach seventh and eighth grade students Spanish.

I was quickly glad that I had not committed to a full term. Their program placed little attention on the spoken word; instead, the focus was on grammar and spelling. This, of course, is 180 degrees off the approach that brought me my success in the teaching field. Seeing that the school was wed to approaching foreign languages through grammatical construction, I didn't feel bad about saying I was not interested in continuing to teach at Westminster and returned to Emory more dedicated than ever to expanding my classes there.

My other connection with Emory is serving as a volunteer docent at the Carlos Museum, which is well known for its collections of Egyptian, Greek, Roman and Ancient America artifacts. I learned a great deal of history while going through the three months of training required to conducting tours. In turn, I find it rewarding, passing on what I have learned.

One of my fond memories of my days at the Carlos Museum will always be hearing one first grader ask another, "Why don't some of the statues have heads?" A little girl explained, "Somebody *touched*." I couldn't have possibly have come up with a more concise answer.

I also have a connection with the Birmingham Museum in Alabama, not as a docent, but as a donor. In appreciation of my services to Costa Rica, I was given a number of pre-Columbian Costa Rican artifacts. When the Birmingham Museum learned of my collection, they asked to see it. They were impressed with the quality and said they very much wanted me to add my pieces to their collection. I agreed to donate two pieces, including the one they wanted most: a small statue of a shaman that had been carved by the Chorotega tribe more than a thousand years ago. He now has a place of honor in the Birmingham Museum.

1998

The United Nations weapons inspectors and Iraqi President Saddam Hussein begin a battle of wills involving Iraq's refusal to end their alleged weapons of mass destruction programs. According to UNSCOM, Iraq alternately intimidated and withheld information from UN inspectors. Alternately, the US and Britain maintain their commitment to air strikes if Iraqi compliance is anything less than total. By the end of 1998, it is a stalemate. While the Iraqi disarmament crisis is escalating on a global level, the American public becomes galvanized on allegations that President Bill Clinton has had an "improper physical relationship" with White House intern, Monica Lewinsky; and that former Catholic priest Rudolph Kos allegedly molested nine former altar boys in Dallas, TX. All 229 passengers of Swissair flight 111 die when the plane crashes in Nova Scotia. It is the year of *Titanic, Shakespeare In Love,* and *Saving Private Ryan.* Longevity is "in": The Price Is Right airs it's 5,000th episode, Mark McGuire breaks Roger Maris' record 61 home runs in a single season, and Viagra is introduced.

Reunion

In 1998, I felt that the time had come for four friends to reunite. I wished to see the three girls with whom I became so close when we were teenagers in Cuba. Jeanne, Ingrid, Fiona, and I never lost touch, even though we went our separate ways after the war. From time to time, one of us visited another. We also exchanged letters, a few phone calls, and a great deal of e-mails. But the four of us had never reunited since we, one by one, departed Cuba for the next phase of our lives.

Each of these women has her own fascinating story, and I will only give some highlights so that you might see what different paths we took as adults.

Ingrid

Ingrid was the daughter of a very well known and well-to-do German banker. Even though he had transferred much of his personal wealth to New York, he did not feel that was the place for his family. That was because, in the late 1930's, there was growing hostility toward Jewish refugees in the U.S. While he felt his money was safest in the U.S., he had already sent his parents from Berlin to Havana and hoped that it would not prove necessary for him to also move his wife and children there.

Ingrid's father clung to that hope much longer than he should have and, in December 1941, found himself and his family stuck in Marseilles along with thousands of us other would-be Jewish immigrants. Although Ingrid's family held visas for Spain and Portugal, on December 7, 1941, Portugal closed its borders, making the family's visas useless. Like my family, they managed to acquire passage to Casablanca. There, the ship *Serpapinto* picked them up on its way to Cuba. They arrived in Havana via Kingston, Jamaica in mid February 1942. After two weeks in the camp at Tiscornia, they were allowed to join Ingrid's grandparents in their boardinghouse. Being considered "enemy aliens," the men in Ingrid's family had to register with the police. Ingrid recalls that for a *propina* (a tip) and socialization, a policeman came to the boarding-house. She says, "It was a comfortable and amicable process."

Already having a strong foundation in French as well as German, Ingrid quickly mastered Spanish at the American-run school she attended. When she began classes, they set her back a year, requiring her to repeat the sixth grade. That summer, she covered all seventh year requirements and entered school the next year as an eighth grader, the correct class for her age.

Her memories of Cuba run toward her parents' efforts to expose her to the symphony on Sundays when tickets were discounted and, through involvement in the *Asociacion Democratica de Refugiados Hebreos*, her parents exposed her to a livelier social life than my parents chose to make a part of our lives.

Ingrid told me that one of her older friends, Jamie Jose, who was half-French and half-Cuban, once took her to the University of Havana to hear about the *Partido Ortodoxo*. This was Castro's party, which was composed primarily of very idealistic young people who were trying to fight the corruption and poverty of Cuba. Little did they know that this party, which was supposed to save Cuba from Batista's corruption, would bring even greater corruption and poverty to the island nation.

In Cuba, an *extrangero*, an immigrant, was only allowed to work if the company was owned by other *extrangeros* and employed at least 50 percent Cuban labor. Since the diamond processors, who were primarily from Antwerp and Amsterdam, brought their factories to Havana, the diamond business provided a large portion of the job available to Jews. Her father, although a bank director by trade, learned how to be a cutter. The skill involved an expensive training process before anyone became qualified to separate the double pyramid of a diamond into two halves.

Even though Ingrid and I had followed similar routes to freedom ... Marseilles to Casablanca to Tiscornia to Havana ... our paths never crossed until we became members of the *Guias De Cuba*, our Girl Scout Troop. For her, as well as for the rest of us, the troop became the center of our lives.

In 1946, Ingrid and her parents followed her grandparents, who had left for the U.S. two years earlier. Their first stop was Miami, flying aboard a DC 3. After a few days at Miami's Flagler Hotel to sightsee, her family moved on to the Bronx. Ingrid temporarily stayed with one great-aunt, while her parents stayed with another because their apartments were quite small and housing of any kind was difficult to find. They eventually found a sublet on Riverside Drive for the summer. In the fall, they moved to another sublet in Kew Gardens, Queens.

After high school graduation came a procession of jobs and evening classes at the New School for Social Research. In 1948, at a Purim Party that was sponsored by the New World Club, a German Jewish organization, Ingrid met Gerald Altman. Gerry, a German Jew, was then attending Rensselear Polytechnic Institute in Troy. Two years later they were married at the home of her parents, and two years after that, their daughter, Karen, entered the picture. Their second child, Laura, was born in 1960. Later, a son, Andy, completed their family.

At the time of their marriage, both Ingrid and Gerry were moving from one unsatisfying job to another. While he worked toward a Master's degree at Polytechnic Institute of Brooklyn, he repaired IBM office equipment part time. This particular job may have set his career path because Gerry eventually became a very important Silicone Valley engineer, working for Rockwell International, the successor of North American Aviation. His specialty was small computers. Prior to his retirement, he spent 1979 to 1989 planning missions for the NASA Space Shuttle.

Ingrid's education, while periodically interrupted by motherhood, eventually resulted in a Bachelor of Science in Physical Therapy from the University of Southern California, as well as an MA in the same field. Today, she is a nurse, specializing in physical therapy.

Of all four of us, Ingrid is the only one practicing Judaism, regularly attending services at a synagogue. Currently, she is the president of the Downey Chapter of Jewish Women International, while Gerry is involved in the B'nai B'rith's lodge and the automated office he set up for Temple Ner Tamid of Downey, a Reform Judaism house of worship.

Jeanne

Jeanne, who was the smartest of all of us, had spent her early childhood in Germany as the daughter of a wealthy and enterprising businessman. In 1937, he liquidated his thriving artificial flower company and moved his family to France, thinking they would be safe there. However, when France declared war on Germany in 1939, he was interned because of his German nationality. Jeanne and her mother traveled south to a little village near Lyon that was not yet occupied by the Germans. Her father managed to escape and went searching for them. There were visas waiting for them at the American Embassy in Paris that had been sent by their relatives in the United States. Since Paris was occupied, the visas would never be received. They headed for Marseilles, traveling by train, a rickety bus, and on foot. Theirs was a journey similar to the one my family traveled.

While her father attempted getting new visas to any country not involved with the war, Jeanne went to school in Marseilles, just as I did. She and her parents stayed at *St. Barnabé*, a hotel outside of Marseilles. This hotel was the headquarters of a highly organized Jewish machine that managed to acquire visas for Jewish families. Every night a new group left for Cuba, Venezuela, Argentina, Chile, or Brazil.

In 1942, when Jeanne was ten, her family was finally able to buy visas and passage on the *Heridian*, a French ship sailing for Casablanca. Although Jeanne's U.S. relatives owned S&W Food Factories and Cafeterias, their wealth was of no help to them in obtaining assistance through U.S. Government channels. Nonetheless, Jeanne and her parents managed to obtain visas and purchase passage aboard the *Serpapinto*, which was a Portuguese freighter that was headed for Cuba. It was the Portuguese freighter's last trip to Cuba, just as my family had sailed on the *Santa Maria's* last trip to Cuba.

Aboard the *Serpapinto*, Jeanne and Fiona met. The two became inseparable. Eventually, through our Girl Scout Troop, the two of them connected with Ingrid and with me.

In 1945, Jeanne's relatives in the U.S. were finally successful in obtaining U.S. visas for her and her parents. The three of them flew to New York for a tearful reunion with her father's relatives.

Jeanne finished high school in the U.S. and enrolled in the University of Wisconsin in order to major in Romance languages and learn Russian. She was already fluent in German, French, Spanish, and English.

At college, she met Anad. He was seven years her senior, a native of Bombay (Mumbai), and working toward a masters in business. This handsome young man fell deeply in love with the beautiful girl with light brown hair, a lovely figure and twinkling hazel eyes. She was fascinated with him, as well. Her father wasn't. Like mine, he hired a private investigator to learn more about this man his daughter wanted to marry. The investigator dug up nothing her father could object to, other than the fact that Anad's ideas of a woman's place and Jeanne's stubborn streak were no ideal match. Her father was upset afresh when Anad announced that he wanted Jeanne to travel to Bombay for the marriage so that they could be joined according to the customs of his family. That's when her father put his foot down. Jeanne could not leave the U.S.A. unless she was married. And, her father more or less got his way. They were married in a civil ceremony in the U.S.

Shortly after their honeymoon, they left for India where Anad started a profitable import/export business. He and Jeanne, despite their conflicting ideologies and religious backgrounds (he is a non-practicing Hindu), have a happy marriage, two children and two grandchildren, all of whom were reared in the western culture. Anad became president of the World Trade Organization in India and is among the country's top five percent in wealth. Jeanne uses her translation skills and secretarial skills to aid a number of charities. Work and pleasure often bring them to New York. They keep an apartment there, as well as their home in India.

Fiona

The most interesting of us all was the one I shall call Fiona. For reasons of her own, she does not want her real name in print. Fiona was younger than the rest of us and had vivid green eyes. Her mother was Italian and her father was French, with a Jewish heritage.

I remember him well because he, like my father, was very much a womanizer. Even more so. His comments to us girls were peppered with double entendres, the second meaning of which always had a sexual connotation. He even showed me a book on sexual positions to test, I presume, my reaction. While the other girls called me boy crazy, I was definitely not interested in older men, and I believe he clearly got the message. Perhaps the evidence of those feelings may have been just about all that caused him to keep his hands to himself. Seeing that I was, however, quite interested in art, he gave me some prints of works by artists such as Van Gogh and Cezanne. I still have the prints stored among the possessions I cherished as a young girl.

In Paris, Fiona's father had owned and run an art gallery, one famous for the great artists who exhibited there. Among them were Picasso and Matisse. The family's friends also included the poet Artaud and scores of lesser known painters and writers. During the war, the Vichy Government of France, the same government that turned over more than 80,000 Jews to the Nazis, confiscated the thriving gallery. Like my father, Fiona's father faced the necessity of getting his wife, daughter, and son to safety. Also, like Papa, Fiona's father managed to buy the necessary visas and passage out of France to Cuba. They were able, fortunately, to take with them some of the family's most cherished paintings. I recall, as a teenager, thinking the ones that were from Picasso's cubist period were simply hideous. My tastes, however, have matured.

After the war, when Fiona was sixteen, the family returned to France, fought for and received, restitution of their gallery. It still exists today. For Fiona's family, life resumed a close approximation to the one they had led before the war, including moving with the crème de la crème of the art world. Regretfully, memories of the flight to safety never leave people who have been driven from their home.

Fiona's tastes leaned more toward adventure than toward schooling. The romantic side of her life has always been her personal blend of ecstasy and chaos. Fiona married a Jewish man and had two children by him. Following a divorce, she became involved with an Arab, whom she did not marry; however, he fathered her third child. From there, she proceeded through a series of affairs. One, I recall, was with a man she claimed was a sheik. One thing is for certain: he was young enough to be her child. Let it never be said that Fiona lacked lasting beauty and a taste for the offbeat.

When she was a teenager, Picasso painted a portrait of Fiona. She eventually sold the painting for a million dollars, a sizeable portion of which she spent acquiring a house and land outside of Giverny, Monet's home. From my one visit there, I recall the old farmhouse had been given an impressive, ultramodern interior. The other paintings she inherited have afforded her the funds to do pretty much as she pleases.

As teenagers, we four girls lived in the same Havana neighborhood and could bike to one another's homes. Our common tie was our participation in Scouts because, unlike Ingrid and Jeanne's families, Fiona's and mine were not practicing Jews. The closeness of our ages and having had many similar experiences helped create the bond we experienced in our all-European troop. While some of the wealthy Cubans invited us to spend time with their daughters at their country homes, we were still outsiders who stayed primarily to ourselves.

Over the years, I made an effort to stay in touch with the others. On occasion, we saw one another one-on-one, however, never as a group. It was time for that to happen; so, in 1998, I contacted Jeanne, Ingrid, and Fiona, concerning a reunion, and received positive responses from all three.

But, where should we meet? Two of us lived in the United States, one in India, and the fourth in France. It seemed obvious to me; the reunion should take place in Cuba. The only problem, of course, was the difficulty of U.S. citizens legally getting to and from Cuba. Frankly, it took some doing for Ingrid and me to stay just inside the legal line of what can and cannot be done; however, we managed to walk the red tape like a tight rope and once again found ourselves together in Havana. For Jeanne, traveling from Bombay and Fiona traveling from Paris, there were no serious travel restrictions. The others joined Ingrid and me at Havana's new airport, and we headed for the National Hotel, a grand structure and still Havana's finest. It had been built by the Mafia and was a great draw for tourists from the U.S. when we were young. We chose to make our reservations there because, as young girls, we had spent many hours watching the rich and famous arrive and leave this palace of a hotel. Now, it was our turn to step inside.

We checked into our two double rooms, one for Fiona and Jeanne, and another for Ingrid and me. Inside the hotel, you felt you were in the lap of luxury. Obscenely lavish food, great service, and every temptation imaginable were there to be enjoyed – all but one. The famous *Cuba Libres* that we had thought the height of sophistication in our teens are no longer served. One reason is Coca-Cola is banned there, and the name of the drink would be looked on as a sad joke; it translates as *free Cuba*. There is, however, a reasonable facsimile served, made with a local cola. But we passed on it. After all, Fiona had brought champagne and pastis for our first night's celebration.

As in the 1940's, Havana remained a city with predominantly two classes: the very rich and the very poor. Looking back on our reunion visit, I gather that most tourists see nothing of Cuba except the glamorous side, predominantly along the Malecon, Havana's wide seaside avenue. We, however, saw much more. Knowing our way around the city, we saw the rest.

I, also, saw a Fiona who was quite different from the delightful girl I used to know. I felt that the Fiona I saw, when the four of us reunited, was a sad and angry person. She had never been maternal and was constantly plagued by wanderlust, which I can understand up to a point. However, I had never seen the sadness before or so much uncontrolled anger. Ever the adventurer and ever blunt, Fiona told the rest of us that we lead very boring lives, compared to hers, and she frequently referred to herself as a "free spirit." That she was, assuming a free one can also be an unhappy spirit. She told us we had no bond, as far as she was concerned. The past was the past, a situation in which fate had thrust the four of us, nothing more. The rest of us did not agree. We were survivors and had gathered to celebrate the fact and revisit our past.

While I felt genuinely sorry to see Fiona living such an empty life with no close ties, the day came when I had a bit too much of her condescension concerning the contrast of her "freedom" with the "burden" of our family ties and dedication to causes. I asked her, "What have you accomplished with your life, Fiona? So, you've traveled with various tribes in third world countries, but you've never done anything with the information you gathered. Nothing to help those people. You've seen the world and certainly had your share of lovers, which is fine by me, but what do you leave the world as your legacy?"

She had little with which to counter, and the tension mounted. Nearly everything any of us suggested doing was too mundane to spark her interest. Much of our exploring of present-day Havana involved just Jeanne, Ingrid, and me.

I deeply wish Fiona had gone with us the day we decided to see if we could find the places each of us had once called home. Fond memories mixed with heartbreak as we made our way through a city that was dirty beyond description. The once exclusive and lovely Vedado and Miramar sections of town are now desecrated and unkempt. The few exceptions are buildings inhabited by Castro supporters. Money pours in to conserve them.

As we walked the hot, humid streets of our past, we discovered that Fiona's home had been torn down, and that we could not locate mine. We did, however, find Jeanne's and Ingrid's. They had lived in the same building. From the outside, it seemed in good repair; so, we decided to knock on the door of what had been Ingrid's home, introduce ourselves to the current tenant, and ask if we could simply look inside for old times' sake? When we knocked, an attractive, well-dressed woman in her mid-thirties answered the door. We explained why we were there, and she graciously invited us in – at the same time, cautioning us to speak in hushed tones because a member of the police lived directly below her apartment.

The woman told us her name was Maria and that she was a doctor. We discovered she was eager to talk to us. She said that her husband, who was also a physician, and their two small children, ages two and five, were expected to survive on their income from the government. Each of these two physicians was paid twenty dollars a month. When we said we couldn't understand how they could afford a nice apartment – much less survive – on $480 a year, Maria started to cry. Through her tears, she candidly told us the rest. "To live any sort of life, my husband and I work as prostitutes at night, servicing the clientele of the hotels that cater to tourists."

Even though we knew that prostitution was a major tourist draw and had learned that children start as early as 14, we were stunned. I think Fiona would have been startled, as well, to learn that professional people had to stoop to this level to survive. The doctor continued volunteering details about her family's predicament. "We have to split the one hundred-dollar fee we each charge with the police. As long as we do, we are free to come and go as we please."

All of us learned more about the Cuban's dilemma from a conversation with Katia, a retired professor with a Ph.D. in history. She admitted, "Yes, I believed in the revolution. In 1959, I followed him (*no one mentions Castro's name*), but he sold us down the river." She added, "Now, we have to beg in the street for menial things such as soap, aspirin, shampoo, and pens."

This lady was a friend of Fiona's, and to Fiona's credit, she helped Katia supplement her meager pension. For some years, Katia had mailed volumes from her valuable library to Fiona, who would in turn sell them in Paris, then go through the complicated process of getting the proceeds from the sale to Katia in U.S. dollars. The money was sent in U.S. currency because the Cuban currency is virtually worthless, and the country operates on a cash economy. Not even the grand hotels accept credit cards.

There is a troubling postscript to this part of our story. After we left, Fiona never heard from Katia again. We have no idea whether she died, or was imprisoned for associating with us, or what. Human life carries little value in Cuba, unless you are a party member.

The young boys who waited on us at the beach were also willing to talk when they felt they weren't being watched. When we asked one of them what he planned to do with his life, he said, "See that ocean? Ninety miles away is freedom. First opportunity I'm getting the hell out of here."

One night we decided we wanted to go to a restaurant that we had read about as being simply wonderful. However, we had great difficulty finding a cab driver willing to drive us to it. We had to settle for a ride to the nearest street corner. Inside the restaurant, we chatted with the owners and learned they had been blacklisted for some minor infraction. When in the police's good graces, they had to split their income with the police and still were not allowed to serve either red meat or lobster. Fish, chicken and vegetables were their limits. What we did have was, nonetheless, delicious. Another night we ate at the *Floridita* Bar, where John and I were married.

There were other surprises and disappointments. While the buildings the two billion tourists per year see along the Malecon waterfront are truly splendid, thanks to a UNESCO grant for their restoration, they are nothing more than facades. Behind them is squalor. Behind the exquisite exteriors, people live with no running water and no electricity. Downtown Havana is in shambles. Grand buildings are falling down from lack of repairs, the streets are an obstacle course of potholes, and the vast majority of the people – skilled and unskilled – live in abject poverty. The debris-filled street drains cause flooding, which in turn erodes the aging building foundations. Consequently, major structures continue collapsing at a rate of one a month. Electricity runs in different sections of the city at certain times but never throughout the day and night. And yet, colorful signs and banners proclaim *The Dream Must Continue ... Che Guevarra's Revolution Was Not in Vain ...We Will Conquer.*

But, no one believes it. Ninety percent of the Cubans will tell you that they are fed up with Castro and Communism. If ever a country was a prime example of the ravages of Communism, Cuba is that country. Castro has destroyed his homeland in a vain attempt to save face.

Tourism and agricultural products they can grow and process, such as sugar, rum, coconuts, and cigars, were Cuba's primary products when I was a girl, and they remain the country's only hope. Tourists do come in large numbers, especially from France, Germany, Italy, and Canada, to enjoy the great hotels and fabulous beaches; however, few come from the U.S., which used to be Cuba's primary market for all it has to offer.

You wonder: who supports Castro and his Communist regime? Out of eleven million inhabitants, perhaps he has a following of 100,000. All are in the military, tourism, or other related fields controlled by his government. There have been five documented attempts on his life.

Perhaps an overthrow similar to Romania's will take place. There, the butcher known as Ceusescu was turned on and killed by his own troops. When the Communist government is eventually overthrown, a democratic government could rebuild Cuba in a matter of years. It's only a one-hour flight from Miami and could reestablish a thriving economy based on its natural products and tourism.

Despite the poverty and misery that surrounded us, we four did have our good times together, as we took our trip down a memory lane that largely no longer exists. We reminisced, we joked, and there was a great deal of kidding me about being the "boy crazy" one when we were teens. We enjoyed delicious dinners at the restaurants for tourists and explored the sections of town no tourist was supposed to ever see. The total experience reaffirmed how important friendships are and how worthy of the investment of our time, energy, and concern necessary to maintain them.

Looking Forward

In 2003, I received the prestigious Kiwanis International Award of the Year. People, such as Olympic visionary Billy Payne and trend-setting architect John Portman, who gave Atlanta and other cities around the world their sleek futuristic appeal, have received this award for their roles in transforming Atlanta into an international city. I am particularly proud of having been included in their company because, in 1991, I was one of the Kiwanians who championed the creation of this special recognition.

I continue my teaching at Emory and supervising the other Spanish instructors in the college's continuing education program. I also have my renewed teaching contract with Yerkes National Primate Research Center, to teach Spanish – No, not to the monkeys! – to the technicians who supervise the Mexican workers. The program emphasizes the importance of certain commands, such as: "Danger! Wear gloves and goggles," which translates "*¡Peligro! pongase guantes y lentes.*"

I walk several miles a day, which gives me time to think and plan. I enjoy my daughters, my grandchildren and most especially the love of the man with whom I've spent 56 years of my life.

In spite of my pathetic swimming skills, twice each month (weather permitting), we head for the Gulf of Mexico to sail in our 37-foot sailboat *Joie de Vivre*. He is the captain; I am "Dammit Rose."

John is my true love, my best friend, my balance, and my safe port. We are bound by time, by habit, by love; he is part of me as much as I am part of him.

I put my translation skills and international expertise to use when called upon, and keep up my friendships with the famous and not-at-all famous. I continue to be a volunteer docent at Emory's Carlos Museum, which specializes in archeological finds, especially those from Egypt, Italy, and Greece, and ancient America.

It is now, 2004. This book is finished. My passionate life is far from over. The Carlos Museum has given me a new challenge - to raise 2.7 million dollars for the acquisition of a valuable Pre-Columbian Ceramic Collection.

Ashley is graduating from high school and my gift to her is a round trip ticket to Paris and another visit to Port Manec'h. She is begging me to return with her – and I am tempted to return because I am always looking forward to life's next opportunity and experience. That's how I have lived; that's how I will continue.

May your life also be filled with a passion for living, an unequalled "*Joie de Vivre*."

Previously Published Articles
by Rose Cunningham

"I Tried Bullfighting in Madrid, Spain"
Atlanta-Journal Constitution Magazine
May 27, 1962

"The Odyssey of the Little Gold Bottle"
The Refresher Magazine
October, 1963

"My Paris Adventure with Alexander" *
Atlanta-Journal Constitution Magazine
May 31, 1964

"Costa Rica Discovery" *
Atlanta-Journal Constitution Magazine
April 18, 1965

"A Day at the Farm with Governor Carter and President Figueres"
Atlanta-Journal Constitution Magazine
June 11, 1972

"Can Atlanta Go International ?"
Atlanta-Journal Constitution Magazine
November 21, 1971

"Traveling in Japan"
Atlanta Magazine
November, 1971

"Lake Como Visit"
Recommend Magazine
February, 1987

* excerpts were used